The Road Home:

A Light In The Darkness

By
Phyllis E. Leavitt M.A.

Dedication

This book is dedicated to the Loving God who filled these pages, to the sacredness of our human journey here on earth, and to Mother Earth who calls to us to all Return Together.

Acknowledgments

I want to give thanks my husband Richard Jenkins for his precious love, his never-ending support, and his belief in my book through all the ups and downs of writing. To my three children, for the gift of being allowed to love deeply and learn so much in this life together. To my daughter Isabella Konold, who has been on an inspiring evolutionary journey with me, who has always reflected back the value of my writing, and who has been an amazing editor. To my son Eddie Konold, for the inspiration of his pure heart, ever seeking mind, and unflagging support of my writing and my inner journey. To my son Daniel Konold for the great questions he asked that caused me to think deeper, and for his unconditional encouragement and love. To Katie Konold for her love, support, and affirmation of the value of what has been given to me, and to Brandi Konold for her love, support and openness.

I want to thank my dear friends Helaine Foster, Aggie Damron, Anne Lewis, Charlotte Taft, and Paul Rossano for their soulful interest and enthusiastic belief in my writing and the path we walk together. Thanks to Dave Garner for his amazing skills in formatting my artwork.

I want to thank my parents, Fran and Jay Leavitt, for their great emphasis on education and the value of writing, and for the lifetimes we have travelled together to find Light in the Darkness.

I will never be able to express enough gratitude to Tom Bird of Sojourn Publishing for the power of his belief in my writing and for all the guidance and support he has so generously given me. I would not have written this book without him. And special thanks as well to Rama of Sojourn Publishing for his expertise and guidance in the publishing process.

The Morning Prayer

I bow to myself
I bow to the Guru within
And the Guru without
Who are one and the same

I bow to all that is
All that was
And all that will be
With Supreme Surrender

I am not afraid
I step willingly
And with a pure heart
Out of the way

And I have faith in God
And in my own soul
Who are one and the same.

Introduction

The Road Home: A Light In The Darkness is a gift that was given to me. An odd way, perhaps, to talk about the book I have been working on (or not) for the last twenty years. It is the story of my personal journey from Darkness into Light, from being absolutely no one in particular—a lonely, depressed single mother with a history of abuse—to becoming exactly the same person but reborn into a different consciousness of not only myself but also the Universe. In one sense this book is the story of my personal deliverance out of suffering and desolation. But that is not the heart of my book.

On December 10, 1994, I had a remarkable experience. I was in therapy, deep in the darkness of terrible memories from childhood. I was as far from any sense of the Divine as I would have thought possible, when suddenly a delicate, rhythmic, otherworldly vibration of light began to pulsate in my forehead. Love and life-giving energy vibrated down my throat and into my heart. Golden light filled me. Then the vibration enveloped me from the outside, rippling in huge waves around my entire body. I heard this message, *"There is a God. This is God and this is how you know God."* The same voice said, *"Surrender totally. Surrender everything-- your pain, your practice, your children, your preconceptions of how things should be and what should happen. Surrender your life. Give it to God."* Golden light shone down from a point inside the top of my head. Then *"Nothing is yours. This is how you find happiness. I'm showing you the Way. In this moment, it is golden and completely unobstructed. You will carve the*

Way out of the stones and dirt of real life experience. It will not always look golden, but remember this. Don't ever look at life the same way again. Make Surrender your practice."

God spoke to me. Although I believed in the God within and I had prayed for God's help, I was totally unprepared to have that prayer answered. On that day, my personal journey unexpectedly became the doorway into another realm. Three months later this voice of God returned and wrote through my hand as I was writing in my journal. After that, all I had to do was ask a question and God and Soul would be there immediately with answers that blew open my "educated" East Coast mind and the limited pictures of healing I had hoped to achieve. "They" had something to say that went way beyond my personal trials and challenges. They had something to say to all of us human beings about what we are doing here in human form, what the Soul purpose is behind all our struggles, and how we can participate in Return to Oneness through the transformation of the exact challenges we face.

As miraculous as it was to hear messages from a Divine Source, it was also very frightening. The fear was that people would think I was either full of myself or a little nuts. Who does she think she is? How presumptuous! *I* was afraid I was a little nuts! All I can tell you is that everything in this book is much larger and more universal than anything Phyllis Leavitt is capable of, much more Divinely Loving and Wise than anything Phyllis Leavitt could or would ever want to take credit for herself.

I was 47 at the time the writing began. I had lived all my life with an unidentifiable pain that would not let me go. I could be sitting in your living room, smiling and having a respectable conversation, but I couldn't connect to anything but my own pain. That was what life was like for me before this Light turned on, before I was shown that within the agonizing disconnection and fear, *my Soul was waiting to reveal the Divine meaning and purpose of it all.*

God's Light did not rescue me from anything lying in my path, but even so, I was changed forever. I was set on a road. I call it the Road Home.

It was an unusual miracle. My Light not only lit up the Darkness I was living in, it wanted to tell me about it. *It walked me through the very same landscape I had been stumbling my way through in the dark again,* but this time the consciousness of my Soul was my loving guide. I had already done many years of therapy. I thought I had gone as far as I could go into the underworld of myself, but I was taken down once more while the Light was held steadily for me, even when I lost my faith, again and again.

God wanted me to understand the nature of what we call Darkness from its Divine point of view. Darkness was not considered an obstacle to Light or that which man has created in defiance of God. God did not judge the Darkness or anything it revealed as evil, stupid or sinful, any more than you would call the rock you stumbled over in the dark a sign of your unworthiness, failure or a fall from grace. Rather, I was very lovingly shown that *the trials we face as we strive to answer our deepest callings are the exact raw materials needed for the Road Home to Oneness,* that what we consider Darkness can be experienced as the doorway to Light. I was shown that the very pain we try so hard to deny, judge or fix is the *food* we eat for the journey, that our greatest difficulties are exactly what we came here, *at our own Soul's bidding,* to transform into Light.

God helped me see that no one is less worthy, less able or less loved in the eyes of Oneness — no one. The message was that we all have the ability to uncover our Divine Nature and experience God directly within the particulars of our own individual trials, triumphs and even within what we consider our failings — and sometimes particularly within what we consider our failings. That is where I began, deep in the pain of all I considered wrong with me. I truly believed that my painful marriage, difficult divorce, loneliness, and inability to find joy had branded me as unlovable. That was where I was when Light found me.

I don't live in that darkness anymore but it's not because I'm special or more worthy or because I have "arrived." My journey, you will see, has been unbearably imperfect, achingly human, and still is. I am a *student* of what was shared with me, not a *master* in any way. And that may be one of the greatest blessings of all. The needs for perfection, self-denial, strict adherence to dogma or beliefs of any kind, are not requirements on the road I took.

For many years I had followed different teachers and tried a number of spiritual practices, but my experiences never seemed to fit any of the prescribed paths. Eventually, I found myself turning within again, with nothing external left to hold onto. And it was then that They appeared and a Road Map was given. It is a Road Map anyone can follow.

The God I found lovingly and patiently walked me through a frightening journey covering lifetimes, all the while showing me how it was that my Soul came cloaked in this person Phyllis and why I faced the particular trials of my particular life. Through that journey, I was shown the bigger picture of *what Soul intended by taking on human form in the first place*. God wanted to help me convert the pain and challenges of Phyllis's experience into Soul Consciousness and become a vehicle for Divine Love. And in one way or another, each according to his own individual path, that seemed to be the ultimate purpose for us all — to carve out our own place in the expression of Divine Love on earth.

The heart of my book is this-- *the Divine wants to manifest in relationship to us all*. It has a Wisdom it wants to share with human beings. God wants to help us find our way Home. My greatest wish, beyond sharing all the particulars of the Light that was shed on our human journey — my greatest wish is that through these pages, the Divine Love that was given so freely to me will vibrate in your heart and light your way.

***

There is no way to fit all of my writing into one book, so this book is the first of several. What is written here is, in some ways, an introduction to the building body of knowledge and understanding about our Soul's journey here on earth as it was shared with me.

PART I

Chapter I — The Fall Part I

I *'m in my bed, or I was just a minute ago. But not anymore. I'm floating up on the ceiling of my bedroom. I love it up here. The little girl who is me is under the covers in her flannel pajamas but I can't see her. It's too dark. I love it up here. I don't want to come down, but sometimes as soon as I have that thought, I'm back inside her in my bed and I feel sad.*

That might be where I start my story. I have never actually found the beginning so this will have to do. You might be wondering what I was doing up on the ceiling, what would drive a little girl out of her body in the night. I never wondered at all. There was no wondering back then. Things just were the way they were.

I guess my family looked good, and I'm not saying there wasn't a lot of good. I think we looked like a normal family in a normal house on a normal street and perhaps we were... Perhaps... But I'm going to tell you the way *I* remember it.

I don't want you to think it was all bad. It wasn't. We had Friday night Sabbath in the dining room with candles and roast beef and potato kugel. We all said the Sabbath prayer in Hebrew (never mind that we had no idea *what* we were saying). We had pajamas warming on the radiator after a bath and the lavender smell of Yardley's on my father's shaving brush in the early mornings. We went to the ocean every summer and ate lobster and ice cream, gathered starfish and crabs. We went to museums and the library and Broadway plays. We bought our clothes in department stores and our front yard was always mowed in the summer. And we had a big wooden workbench in the basement where my older brother drew long-legged birds that fit into each other like Escher paintings, where he taught my sister and me block printing and silkscreen making and copper enameling.

But there were signs, too, that all was not right. At least all was not right *with me*.

I'm playing school in the den. I take out a black and white composition book from the shelf in the corner. I start out practicing my ABC's and drawing the same little house with yellow curtains in the windows, but I'm not practicing my ABC's now. I'm not doing math either. I'm drawing someone who hurts little girls. Just the face and a little bit of what they did. I can feel the hurt when I draw it. I don't know why I do it. I know there is something all wrong about drawing these pictures, that I don't want anyone to see them, but I have to draw them anyway. I close the book and hide it under the crayons and colored pencils.

She never drew the whole thing. She didn't know what the whole thing was. All I know is that she was waking up at night with those images of someone hurting a little girl long before she drew them. I don't think she even knew the little girl was her. In fact, I know she didn't.

So I think there were signs. It's hard to imagine in all the years we played in that den that no one ever saw those pictures and wondered what the hell I was doing.

I was afraid of the dark by the time I was two or three. If the light is on, you can see the spiders before they get you. I *could not* go to sleep if the hall light wasn't on, and the entire bedroom had to be checked for spiders. I watched the light slide across the cold wooden floor, waiting for the slightest shadow of hairy legs. If there was a spider, my father had to take it away. I spent an entire summer at Girl Scout camp refusing to sit on the log to eat lunch with the other children, just sure a spider would find me.

You see, you obsess about spiders because there is a possibility of keeping spiders from crawling on your skin, whereas your skin itself — well that's a whole other can of worms. There is no hall light that can protect you from a feeling of burning, crawling flesh when there is no fire visible. There are no words to scream because there is no understanding in the mind and no throat that could open anyway to call for help. Tell me, how do you get out of your own skin if that is where all the terror congregates?

Well, I'll tell you– you don't. You *don't* get out of your skin. So you go away. You find every way imaginable for a human being to go away from her own skin. You hate sweating because it reminds you, so you make sure not to do anything that makes you sweat. You suck in your stomach, suck in your breath, and suck in your eyes until they roll back into that smoking black oven in your own head with only just enough vision turned outward to steer you down the steps or across the playground. Then you crawl somewhere even further inside where there is no skin, no sweat, and no little girl.

Nobody sees a thing, not one bit of you colors itself outside that tightly drawn line, and not one bit of you comes out of *that* hiding place where spiders *crawl on you anyway*.

So you see there was this odd juxtaposition of realities long before anyone talked about things like "reality" or the psyche or extrasensory perception, at least in my neck of the woods back in the 50's and early 60's. There was the reality we all acknowledged, the one you could see like the big oak tree in the front yard, the overstuffed armchair my father sat in to listen to his classical music, and the little white porcelain shoe dotted with pink and green flowers on the knick-knack shelf. There were neighbor kids we played jump rope and hopscotch with, the Catholic Martins who had a huge Christmas tree every year and bowls full of ribbon candy we could take without asking. And there were the stunning red/green iris tips that poked their little heads up along the driveway every spring of every year even before the winter air was gone.

And then, well, then there was the other reality that was not seen but only swallowed, like time-release poison in your innocent little grape soda, that shadow world where someone hurts you in a basement, where horror explodes out of the dark and scorches your *very* little girl body, and then retreats without a trace into the night, where it can jump out on spider legs and get you when the lights go out.

Juggling all that becomes a way of life, as automatic as breathing, as second nature as tying your shoes. You become accustomed to the sound of nails scraping across a chalkboard while the rest of the world seems to be hearing music, and so you do your best to act as if you are hearing music, too.

Don't misunderstand. It's not like all the juggling works! You don't *hear* music. You just go mute, you just go numb, and you wade your way through sleepovers and birthday parties like a loon in an oil slick. The older you get, the more complex it becomes. There is an outside you and an inside you. You hide the inside you. You stuff her back in and you stuff her back in because she just doesn't belong, and you *know*, without knowing anything, that there is something very wrong with her. And so despite the bubble baths and despite blowing out the Hanukah candles with their beautiful colored wax dripping down the stem of the Menorah just before bed, the little girl that was me lay under the covers sleepless and saw herself buried alive in a coffin, imagining herself in the bottomless black nothingness of death. Or she lay there in terror of the house burning down, she up there on the second floor agonizing that there was no ladder outside her window, because what if... while her parents watched television and ate mocha chip ice cream in the den downstairs.

Those were the silent cries. That was the Wilderness I lived in for as long as I can remember. The Fall from Grace was as soundless as spider footsteps. Not all the cries were silent though. There were many that were long and loud, some in the daytime and some in the middle of the night. They let her "cry it out" in the daytime. I can't imagine what she did that was so bad, but I hear my mother downstairs letting my father know exactly how upset she is with me. She shrieks in her I-can't-take-it-anymore, it's-your-fault-Jay, half-helpless, half-accusing voice.

She's calling me a witch.

At night, I imagine my cries made it impossible for them to sleep and so eventually, I would hear my father's footsteps on the stairs. To this day, I have not one memory of him entering my room.

So you see there are two realities, one outside and one inside. The outside you is always on the lookout. It has to make sure the inside you *never* shows. And so, in a way, *you are always outside yourself*, but of course you don't know that either. You don't know anything. You just try to be good and get all your homework done.

So let me just say this. If it isn't entirely clear *what happened*, that's because it *wasn't*. You know a heck of a lot more than I ever knew back then, because I knew nothing.

Chapter II — The Fall Part II

I can tell you I was not ready when the whole boy thing hit me. Believe me; I was *not* ready for the boy thing. I think I was in sixth grade when Bobby came over one day looking for my brother. I must have been home alone and I let him in. All I remember now is the sun coming through the living room windows and Bobby kissing me and sticking his tongue way down into my ear. I could not make myself move. My mouth did not open to say no, my feet were rooted to the floor, and my head did not pull away from his mouth. You might say I must have wanted him to kiss me, but I didn't because it made me sick. Then he left and the afternoon sank into the gray oblivion that seems to be left in the wake of that kind of undistinguished paralysis.

I was not ready for breasts or girls who had them. All my friends were the Jewish girls I went to Saturday School with. They were, every one of them, beautiful and smart and popular. They all got their periods long before me. I watched from my frozen place on Mars as they filled out their bras, painted their eyelids blue and green and slid easily into stockings, waved their cheerleader pom-poms and got into cars with boys, while the body I was trying so hard *not* to inhabit kept walking down the halls of my Junior High School thinking about my homework and if the socks that matched my sweater were clean.

It's a fair walk to Junior High. I walk it alone. My brother is in High School now and my sister is still in elementary. I have a blue scarf on my head to keep the humidity from turning my carefully hair-sprayed hair to frizz and I'm carrying a huge pile of books. I'm walking on West Eighth Street now, several blocks up from my house. Across the street is that enormous pink azalea hedge, but it isn't blooming now. A man in a tan car passes by me very slowly. I wonder if he knows me. The car keeps going. But oh, he must have gone around the block because here he comes again. He pulls to the curb right beside me.

You have to understand that I was very nearsighted but I hated the way I looked in glasses so I refused to wear them except in class. I can't see who he is.

*He must know me. He must be a friend of my parents and he wants to give me a ride. I walk to the car. I reach my hand out to grab the door handle. I am about to get in. **He must be a friend of my parents**. **He wants to give me a ride**. Now, even without my glasses, I see his face. **I don't know him**. I walk away from the car very fast like I never meant to get in, like I don't know you and I **didn't** walk up to your door.*

I DIDN'T GET IN!!!... I DIDN'T!!!

And that was how I remembered the man in the car. That was in fact my memory for most of my life until the earth quaked somewhere in my late forties and up from her boiling depths I vomited the man in the car out of the black wreck of myself, and in the aftershock, Oh God, in the aftershock I saw that even in my original memory, the street I walked away from the car on was *not* West Eighth Street. I walked away from that car somewhere around the corner, not on the route I took to school. How could that be? Yet, *I **always** knew that, even as I **never** let myself know.*

And that was it. That was probably the last and biggest nail in the coffin. It is beyond me now to even begin to imagine how the rest of that day unfolded. At some point I must have gone home, buried my head in a book, and obsessed about my hair, my clothes, and my grades. I'm quite sure I did. I already knew how to make spider goo disappear. You just study and study more and you make sure you roll your hair up tight every night in rollers the size of logs so that even sleep hurts. The rest becomes a blur. Like a blanket of fog that sits on the earth and only the highest peaks break through the topmost layer– that was the quality of my life. Something dark and impenetrable sitting on top of me all the time, and so the fear of moving becomes even greater because you can't see two feet in front of you. You don't know what is out there, where the road might suddenly drop off all together. Like a blind woman, I traced and retraced the steps that were familiar, where I had some sense of knowing the way, knowing what to expect. I studied and curled my hair and studied and curled my hair and obsessed about my clothes.

I know I tried hard to find rides to school for a while, but even then, I didn't know why. My father left for work early and my mother was still in bed. Soon, even the desperation not to walk to school alone, like everything else, sank back into the fog and disappeared. Somewhere inside that heavy cloud, though, an electrical charge must have built up because one day I just started cutting my hair and I could not stop. When I was done, I had about an inch and a half of hair left on my head, if that much. I don't know how I got myself to school after that. But of course, I went.

And no one said a word. Nothing.

So as I said, I was not ready for breasts or girls who had them. Mine, by the way, refused to graduate from an A to a B cup. So when my friend Beth was already a size D before I even got my period, well, let's just say that didn't help. I had one brief boyfriend in ninth grade. His name was Mel and he was a friend of my best friend Liza's boyfriend Sam. Yes, it must have been no later than ninth grade because Liza and I stopped being friends when Sam became a permanent fixture in her life. She passed through a door that I could not go through. I *wanted* to go through that door but I didn't know how. I was stuck in the waiting room while my friends glided into the ballroom and danced away. Mel kissed me in the back seat of Sam's car. His saliva felt like puke going down my throat and that was the end of boys for me until college. I would start all over again in college. I just knew I could be a very different person and no one would know this old me.

Meanwhile, the electrical charge continued to explode. I ripped off my fingernails. If I "accidentally" bled, well, too bad. The desire to pull at my skin was stronger than the need to keep it intact. That has to be an aberration of nature, don't you think? What amoeba do you see under a microscope that intentionally breaks its cell wall? What flower leans toward the dark? And what would it take, *what would it take,* for a flower to override its natural instinct, turn itself around, and start growing into the shadows?

Well, I guess I've *told* you what caused that.

But you see, that's actually *not* what I want to talk about. There are all kinds of psychological articles and autobiographical accounts of what happens to a person when sexual abuse goes undiscovered and untreated, about repressed memories, self-harm, and difficulties with intimacy and trust. I know that material inside and out as one of millions who have made the journey across the great divide between forgetting and remembering. I know it as a psychotherapist and I know it as a client. And I know that the stamina required for that journey is worthy of the utmost respect. But I'm not here to testify that people really can forget and remember later and I'm not here to testify about the lasting pain of their symptoms. *For me, all of that is a given.*

Chapter III — A Light in the Darkness

I want to tell you something very different about what life is like when you **don't** remember. I want to tell you about the **beauty** as well as the agony, because strangely enough, for me, there has been an exquisite beauty. I want to tell you that burying your truest self at a very early age is perhaps not the very worst thing that can happen to a person, because in the process of looking for wholeness, I found parts of my existence I did not know I had lost, parts I perhaps would not have found had it not been for the extreme terror of the situation.

I can only speak for myself when I say that something had to give. I don't know how this life force works inside us, why it is sometimes so tenacious in the face of poison in all forms, but when it decides to stay here in the body, I guess it just decides to stay. Because believe me, there were so many times I didn't think I had what it took to stay alive. But I have come to believe that our life force is essentially good, essentially beautiful, and unbearably wise. And so when I speak of being split at an early age, I speak not only of the split between the apparently clean, neat surface of my life and the dark festering interior. Something else happens.

The life force itself *goes* somewhere *but it doesn't disappear*. My life force could not live in the front rooms of my house, looking freely out the windows, choosing who and what to let in or turn away. When you've had your front door opened forcibly too many times, or maybe even only once, what is precious and most dear looks for somewhere else to live. It does this all on its own, no thought or planning required. Like an animal hunted in the wild, it does not stay out in the open. Sheer instinct and the basic will to survive take it as far out of view as possible. And so, being stuck as it were in the little house that is your own body, that part of you still has to find a way to move to safer quarters. In my case, I would say that that part of me went out a back window and hovered on the windowsill for many, many years. It was so frightened it couldn't possibly live in the house, and yet it couldn't leave either, because leaving is bodily death. And so it hovered outside a window, still attached but "gone." I will tell you how I came to know this, but that understanding is years in the making and I am not there yet.

For now, I only want to say that this part of me, and I am going to call it my soul, did not always hover just outside my house. It came to me. It let me know it was there. Perhaps it had to, perhaps there is some law that says a soul that came into a body at birth, if disembodied, must be born into it again. And again, and again, until body and soul come back together. I really don't know. And of course, you know I was Jewish and we didn't talk about soul or spirit, so when something came to me for the first time, I didn't have a clue it was really a part of me. I considered it a visitation, a miracle.

Did I tell you we were Reformed Jews? That's the easiest kind of Jew to be. Nothing much is required of you. You don't have to keep Kosher, you don't have to go to Temple, women don't have to cover anything up or sit separately, and the Bar Mitzvahs are more about the party afterwards than any meaning I can remember being given to entering adulthood. I mean really, you can just say you're Jewish and that's enough.

16

We did go to Temple though. Only my brother got Bar Mitzvah-ed. Thank God no one made me go to Hebrew School!

Temple is an old sanctuary with blue velvet cushioned seats, brilliant stained glass windows, monotone sermons and a fashion show of the latest in ladies clothing. "Did you see what Maizie was wearing? Oi, she has taste like the Goyim!"

*We do a call-and-response prayer together as a congregation. Is God calling to us or is it the other way around? I don't know. I'm not listening. **Nothing** there calls to **me** and I respond to nothing.*

That God is somewhere behind a pillar smiting the Assyrians. I can't see his face.

So there was nothing in my experience that I called God. My *soul* first made itself known to me in a poem I wrote as a teenager. I must have been fourteen because I think I had already moved into my brother's bedroom, and that was when he left for Harvard. I was sitting at his old desk and there was a feeling of late afternoon coming through the window that overlooked the driveway and the Melman's house next door. Through my hand, a poem found its way onto a piece of paper and some hidden princess I never knew was there got kissed and woke up. For a few precious moments, the black and white landscape inside me became color. The sun's warm rays reached me for what felt like the first time. I know it sounds melodramatic, that it couldn't have been *that* icy cold and bleak in my little suburban food-on-the-table, complete with new paten leather shoes Plainfield, New Jersey existence, but all I can tell you is that writing that one poem irrevocably changed my life. I was born. Some pink and perfect little being finally made its way out of the womb.

I only remember one line of that poem now — "I fell to my knees by the water." Where those words came from, I will never know. I had *no* experience of reverence of any kind as a child. But my soul must have remembered because it was a deep feeling of reverence that came to me in that poem. I can still feel the flood of awe rising from my heart into my throat when I write those words now.

I was naïve enough to believe that all I had to do was write another poem and I could find that again. But perhaps a certain amount of naiveté is not such a bad thing. I finally knew what it was like to feel alive. And so I "tried" to write poetry. Sometimes, certainly not always, I was able to make that connection again. Maybe my soul came in from the windowsill for a moment, I don't know. That would be my guess. But it didn't take long for me to see that the very pain poetry relieved began to seep out through the images, insisting on a voice, begging for words, muddying up the pages. And so eventually, I burned everything I had written. Don't remember when. Not leaving *that trail* for anyone to follow. Not leaving *that trace* of dirt. No, my room has to be clean. It may be unlivable, but it will look clean.

It's sad really, when what you fear the most lies inside your very own being. It's sad when the only passageway to light takes you to the brink of some black abyss where no one in her right mind would ever want to go. You are simply left uncomprehending, speechless, and afraid, when only words will save you.

Nevertheless, my first glimpse of life came to me through words, and my psyche was not about to forget it. Nor did I abandon that ship altogether. I became an even better student. I

18

wrote a play in school about a little girl in Nazi Germany that was chosen to be performed. I wrote papers that were published in school journals. I studied, wrote, thought, and wrote as much as humanly possible. I kept my mind and my words where they would be relatively safe, in the world of *ideas.*

But I still held poetry sacred, still believed it could take me back to Eden. It was the only God I knew.

So you can see the dilemma in its paradoxical beauty. The miracle doesn't occur without the tragedy; Lazarus had to die before Jesus could bring him back to life. And how could we understand the sun's brilliance if it weren't for the multitude of lightless objects that block its rays? Would I even have known that I *existed* if it weren't for the fact that soul reached for me across the cosmos, found me in a poem, and lit me up in my own solitary orbit around the earth?

The dilemma is that there is no fast track to Nirvana. There is no bypass route around the clogged arteries of your journey. There is no going around; there is only going through. At least that is how it has been for me. Of course, I cannot tell you this is some absolute spiritual truth. Maybe you have had a different journey. Maybe your life has operated under some other set of laws. If so, I count you blessed. I have had to look for my blessings where I could find them, the stunning and unexpected Oasis Cafés that have appeared after miles and miles of waterless landscape.

If your soul lights you up with *words*, if the special at the Oasis Café is *poetry* and you are starving after your proverbial forty years in the desert, and you eat from that plate and drink from that cup, then you *will return* for another helping. When writing is your savior, you cannot help but write. Burning your poems cannot stop that. You cannot turn away from the only hand that feeds you.

And let me tell you, as dark as that night is, God, the dawn is incredible. God, you hold on for more of that and you don't let go, even if you think you want to, even if the "savior" has to take you back down into the basement, back down to your own fall from grace.

And so you find yourself in yet again another war within your apparently quiet middle-class American tree-lined self. You want to write. You want that moment on a sun-baked rock, quiet as a lizard, timeless as his breathing into the hot dry air of creation. You know it is there, right at the tip of your pen, a door that paper and ink open to a long forgotten cosmos you know better than the streets of Plainfield, New Jersey but still cannot remember.

***

Out of all the chaos, there slowly emerges a pattern. I didn't recognize it back then, of course, but it stands out now like the obvious spiral of a spider web, breathtakingly gorgeous when illuminated in early morning sun, deadly to all that inadvertently offers itself up to be devoured. Every visitation, every breakthrough of light revealed some new aspect of the darkness that shrouded me. In the early days, I had no way to interpret this pattern. It simply felt that after a breath of air, feelings of utter alienation and continual loss suffocated me in my bed. I thought I was being punished for believing that love in any form could find me, even for a moment. I know now that isn't true. I know now that soul does not ever punish, that soul is working endlessly to light the way, and if the way is filled with debris, surely it is an act of loving kindness for soul to point that out. But back then I didn't know there was debris. In my poems, I never got beyond a rush of words, like black paint spilled by accident onto a page that was supposed to be white.

And still the dawn came golden every once in while.

I really believed I grew up in a normal household, that the only abnormality was me. I still thought, on some level, that the whole reason for being was to get "A's" in school. The God of my primitive child mind would accept nothing less, but for the life of me, I could not figure how to get an A in the life I was living. The God of my primitive child mind still expected me to marry the nice Jewish doctor and live in a suburban neighborhood with paved driveways and manicured lawns. And there was no way to please that God. I was *not* on the road to suburbia, not that I didn't *want* to be, believe me. But the troupe of girls with teased hair and chiffon dresses and perfect skin were long gone down that elusive highway. Stupid, stupid me, I don't know how I did it, but I missed the turn.

Riding the train from New Jersey to New York during my time at The New School College, I stared at the lit windows of home after suburban home flashing by, the warm yellow light, the imagined sense of belonging, of people sitting down to dinner together, going to bed together, my little soul hovering outside an endless array of windowsills. I see that now. *That* was a part of the pattern, but it was a mystery to me then. And here is where that spilt was so obvious. In my child mind, I desperately wanted to go back to that home I never had; in my adult body, the idea revolted me.

Looking back, I see that somewhere early on the road did indeed fork, and that different parts of me went different ways without conscious knowledge of the discrepancies. What would it have been like to live with all of me conscious inside my heart and mind and body from the very beginning? I cannot tell you. That is not my story. My story is about what happened when my life force was pushed right up against death's door but did not pass through. It is the story of what happens when a consciousness has to go underground to survive, and it is the story of the innate struggle to return to a state of wholeness and integration. But more than that, *much more than that*, it is the story of the particular route I took and the unexpected discoveries I made along the way.

I told you it was the soul that left the body, went out the window, and left my little personality to steer the ship alone. But I'm not so sure of that anymore. I'm not convinced that the soul ever goes anywhere. Perhaps it knew what it was doing all along, coming down here into this mess for the very purpose of extracting some exquisite juice from so many crushed grapes. Maybe soul just takes on a variety of experiences, some "apparently" dark and some "apparently" light, and we are here to make sense out of the puzzle that creates. Maybe we are here to write our own play out of this most dramatic of tensions all held within one body and one psyche. I have been assuming that soul is everything that is not darkness, not pain, but maybe soul is beyond even that: maybe it holds the whole ball of wax. I do assume that there is some kind of intelligence behind all this that we can ultimately understand, even if that understanding is in a constant state of flux and change. Little pieces of my life experience tell me this is so.

My individual heartache is likely no more than yours, and maybe a great deal less, if such things can be measured. So I certainly don't mean to say I've suffered more than most. My suffering, such as it was, was always something I considered a great flaw, an overwhelming liability, so it is not that I particularly enjoy telling you about it. I don't. If I could erase it, if I could tell you I've lived my life in the sun, I would be very relieved. For most of my life, I wished I could have been someone, *anyone*, other than the lost little girl I continually encountered inside me, the one I came to hate and judge mercilessly. I only tell her story because it is an essential part of my truth. Well, no, that isn't accurate. That isn't the *only* reason I tell her story. As much as I might wish I had a different tale to tell, I think I have come to love the one that climbed such a mountain alone and lived to tell about it. I tell it because I don't hate her anymore and in telling her story, I get to listen to all the things she never got to say and therefore could never fully know. I tell it because everything I hated about her has turned to love of her ordeal. You know how children love to hear stories about themselves, about the day they were born or the first time they walked or how brave they were getting stitches? Well, that little girl in me is just like that. She needs to have her story told back to her. It makes her feel real and true.

And if there is one thing I've learned, there is nothing out there apart from my own truth. I ran from it the better part of my life, and I will tell you there is absolutely nowhere to go. It's like trying to run from your own feet. I was either blessed or cursed, depending on how you look at it, with a relentless need to understand myself. Perhaps that is what happens when you live inside a riddle that appears to have no answer and you have no idea how you even got there. And yet, now I would have to say that as lost as I felt, as unaware of traveling any comprehensible road as I might have been, *something took me where I needed to go.*

I'm wondering now if there isn't some innate magnetism that one piece, long broken off from another, has to the place of rupture and therefore to ultimate unity with itself.

What if the force and the urgency of that magnetism is the love of God?

PART II — Looking For God

Chapter I

W hatever I learned about God growing up, it was definitely *not* a force calling out for union. I told you we were Reformed Jews. I can't tell you what Reformed Jews believe in because I don't think I got beyond a basic familiarity with a few Bible stories and the underlying and *very* important principle that the Jews are God's chosen people. The God of my childhood was a towering figure with a beard, long robes, and a staff who looked down from flaming clouds, made rules, and smote those who disobeyed. The God of my childhood was all about right and wrong, about people fighting their petty battles in His name, about not eating pork. I didn't get it nor did I want to. I sat quietly through Friday night services because I learned to sit quietly. I stared at the shine on my new shoes, unbearably passive, waiting for the Oneg Shabbat, for the cake we were given when all that boring Hebrew was over. I was a good girl who knew how to be good and the Jews were the good guys in God's opinion, or so I was told. The Jews supposedly had some unnamed edge over the Egyptians and the Assyrians and whoever else was apparently so determined to be bad, but those heathens got their come-uppins all right, directly from God himself. I just wasn't into it.

When Mr. Lane from across the street died and my parents went to his funeral, it was probably one of the first times they went into a Catholic Church. My mother came home with a look of amused disdain, saying that "the Goyim," really believe that

Jesus personally came for Mr. Lane, forgave his sins, and took him to Heaven. She said it like that, like, "Really, how childish. We Jews don't need *that.*" But what is it exactly that we don't need? We don't need comfort, we don't need a belief in something just a little bigger and more compassionate than what we find here on earth? We don't need a belief in something greater than our very smart, very successful, very ethically correct little selves? We, who have been roasted mercilessly in ovens and scattered unwanted across the earth, we don't need a hand stretched out to us across time and space, we don't need a home somewhere in the afterlife, when so many of our homes have been marked with an X and *so many have been killed*, not just the first born?

The God of my Saturday school and the message from my parents was, look, you are great, you are the smartest and the best; you are the chosen one. But don't look to me to fill that hollow inside your trunk. I don't even want to hear about it. You fill it up with A's and marriage to a nice Jewish man from an Ivy League School. You fill it up with a spotless house and 2.5 children who get A's and go to Harvard and Yale. That's all you have to do to pass this test. Heaven, if you really need one, is new carpeting in the living room, Chinese food on Sunday night, and a car with power steering.

Don't get me wrong, I do not pretend even for an instant that I speak for all Jewish people. I only speak of my experience of the Judaism I was exposed to. Maybe my parents' generation was just too numb from the Second World War and Hitler to even begin to think about a loving God, a God who *could* personally come and deliver you out of the oven or gas chamber, because as far as anyone could see, no such God came. Maybe even the thought that such a God might exist was a slap in the face no Jew could tolerate. How could we be a *chosen* people and be *chosen for that*? Not that I remember anyone discussing thoughts like these in my childhood. I just remember a TV show with photographs from the concentration camps, mountains of skeletons, limbs lying inhumanly askew, piles of gold teeth, glasses, and stone soap. And other images of the still living, eyes glazed over in their blackened hollow sockets, skin stretched over bone faces that had once sat at their own full tables, eating, dreaming, loving, and living.

And not a word said afterwards. The commercial came on and we got ice cream and went to bed.

Easier to laugh at the idea of a personal God, that nervous, judgmental little laugh that covers millions of scourged bodies in an instant and leaves the living room clean and smelling like Lemon Pledge. Not to say that that I blame any Jew, not at all. Who would want to even think about concepts like sin, Hell, confession, and forgiveness? What sins could the Jews have to confess, and what did we need to have forgiven? What Hell could be worse than the one already constructed right here on earth out of bricks, barbed wire and sadists with guns and gas? No, it is very understandable, really, that we did not turn toward a Savior, that we believed even more fiercely in education and intelligence, money, nice houses and schnapps. If God cannot help you in your worst hour of need, if God has no control over the Germans, *and if you are, nevertheless, at the very same time,* so *chosen,* so special, and the belief that God will *someday* smite your enemies doesn't quite cut it, then it only makes sense you are going to believe in something much closer at hand than the dream of a personal God who comes and takes you to Heaven. You are going to believe in something you *can* control, something you have a say over, like your grades or getting into a good school, having the lawn mowed every week and protecting the couch with a plastic cover.

After college I cleaned houses for two women who had survived Nazi Germany, tattooed numbers on their arms, scores of family members lost, stories I never asked to hear. I looked around their houses in awe at the faux antique furniture, porcelain cherubs with pink cheeks and gold wings, murals of ladies with parasols painted on their living room walls, ruffled satin lampshades, and stacks of canned tuna fish and every imaginable non-perishable stuffed into their pantry shelves.

And I thought to myself how unbearable it would be to live in those houses with their fine film of organza and lace draped over the memory of black blood and silenced screams. And yet, now I think I understand. What else, really, would I have them do? What God were they supposed to believe in? And I was no different really, except that for whatever reason, lace and cherubs did not work for me, so maybe they were even better off than I was. I kept seeing a shadow of blood under the organza and so I couldn't put it on. Actually, nothing worked for me, and to tell you the truth, I don't have the faintest idea whether those porcelain cherubs and all the faux finish in the world worked for them either. I'll never know, and frankly, I highly doubt it. I don't doubt for a moment that they, too, woke breathless in the middle of the night, chased savagely by black shapes with knives, feet slipping off the last crumbling foothold before final extinction, night after endless night.

So what if they made their world a blue living room with painted parasols and *very* ersatz Monet. If that's what it takes, if that relieves even one moment of horror, I can respect that. Back then, I couldn't understand it at all, and now I know why. They *remembered* what happened to them and were very happy to forget, if even for an instant at a time. I *didn't*, and so my psyche was both appalled and frightened by the apparent denial of what was tattooed into their arms and splashed in red across their souls. I don't even know what I expected. That they would cry all day or paint their walls black and eat scraps from the trash? No, they had their faux graven images and more power to them! They came out of Egypt with *nothing* but the stripes on their backs. So what if they made a calf out of gold huddled alone in the desert, so what! I think Moses was wrong. I think that God of his was wrong, too.

***

I think our ideas of God are a reflection of where we turn in order to tolerate being our very human, mortal, and incredibly vulnerable sensate selves. I mean, don't we all turn to something — money, work, love, family, education, drugs, food, TV, science, nature, service to others, as well as to religion or spirituality? Don't we make whatever we worship, whatever we believe in, God-like in some way? Don't we adore it, attend to it, put it first, arrange our lives around it and sacrifice for it? Don't we fear the power these things have over us as much as we hold them sacred? Isn't that deification? I wonder now if the ancient Greeks were that pagan after all, with their multitude of deities, Gods of Love, of Hearth and Home, Beauty and Wisdom, Gods of War and the Underworld, Death and Destruction. Maybe they were just a whole lot more honest than we dare to be. Maybe they were able to admit they believed in the power of all these things in a way we still fool ourselves that we don't or that we shouldn't, that our God is something beyond all that worldly stuff.

Even so, here I am with my little story, and I say "little" not to be humble but to be in proportion to the sky. Here I am with my little story of all the Gods I have worshipped, all the golden calves I have created in the middle of my own deserts, all the Gods who have come to meet me on my way and the particular Temples into which I was granted entrance.

Chapter II

I t's 1965. John is one of my brother's best friends. We write to each other the whole summer of my senior year while he and my brother travel around Mexico. John is smart and funny and we trigger a sharp wit in each other that we bat around like a Ping-Pong ball. It's wonderful until I move to Boston for my freshman year in college and we can actually be together, date, go to football games and then be left alone with nobody but ourselves in his dorm room. Lee Goldstein who lives down the hall in my dorm, the impossibly overdone New Yorker with thick black eyeliner and frosted white lipstick, dresses me up in fish-net tights, a short skirt and make-up for one of my dates with John.

I feel naked. I don't know how to do the girl thing, I don't know if I want to do it, my legs all showing. I don't know how to come back into the front rooms of my house.

John and I have some kind of mixed drink that night, not much as far as college drinking goes. I have only part of a glass but it makes me tired. I'm on his bed and he's kissing me. We're only kissing, aren't we? But he gets all agitated and he comes before I can remember what that means.

I can't love him, that's for sure. I can only see his goodness from very far away. And from very far away, I know he will make a great husband and father, but up close, NO. The thought of him near me, I can't, the kind look of longing in his face—I don't want to see it.

We're standing in the courtyard of a Harvard dorm, he is holding me, and I'm crying. I know I won't see him again AND I know exactly what I'm saying no to, which is exactly the life I think I would otherwise want, if something wasn't terribly wrong with me.

I am cast out of Eden before I ever know what really happened. I don't know what apple I ate or what God I have enraged. But here I am, outside its gates where God could not possibly love the little girl who can't accept the nice Jewish doctor-to-be.

***

I'm in my second year of college at Simmons now. I go out one afternoon with my roommate Kate to Boston Commons. The sun is an electric golden glow behind the last autumn flowers perched royally on their stalks in calm anticipation of the frost. Kate and I wander away from each other.

A curtain suddenly rises and I find myself inside the living being of the Earth. I am no different from a flower, a bush. We are all born of the Mother. We are all held together by her electric love. The trees are conscious beings dancing in the wind, their woody arms no different from mine. Every particle of light, every breath of wind, every petal spinning in its ageless flight to the ground is alive and Divine. There is no wind apart from sun apart from tree apart from me. And yet Light is an entity, wind is a conscious presence, earth is a chorus and everyone and everything is included in her ecstatic song. Everyone and everything is calling and responding like the first great chant in the first great hall of the first Great Spirit. The veil of illusion that we are alone here, that all other living things are merely the background

34

*for our human drama, that veil is lifted and for a blessed few minutes, I am **in** the river of life, not standing, aching on the shore.*

And then, just as suddenly, the veil falls and I am back in Boston Commons and Kate is gone to meet a guy. I am alone again as the air gets cool and the sun begins to sink. I look around for a sign, a tangible marker that the ordinary has opened into the extraordinary for one miraculous moment, but there is none. There is only this lonely girl walking her solitary way back from the garden, looking for any sign of love on an empty horizon.

Soul has come for me again. I don't know why it had to leave so soon.

I held onto that sweet taste as long as I possibly could, but my loneliness here was all the more acute. My "visitation" left me more bereft than ever. Of course, I didn't call it a visitation back then. I didn't call it God. It was more like a little blip of light on a radar screen that has always been dark. You found it, you located its coordinates at last and then the screen again goes blank and you are left awed, grateful beyond measure and desolate all in the same breath.

You see, I was just clinging to life any way I could by that time. I think it wasn't long after that experience that I kind of cracked up, at least as close to cracking up as I could without going all the way.

I was reading poetry for a literature class at Simmons, images of a night sky and musings of man's place in the universe, something like that. I know this probably sounds crazy, or maybe this is what crazy really is, but I went out into that night sky somewhere in my psyche and I couldn't get back, like a child's balloon that floats all the way out of earth's atmosphere but doesn't burst, a bright plastic bubble that has no meaning away from a toy store or a birthday party, has no connection to a hand holding its string.

I try to go on functioning but I can't. I go to my college adviser, an old man with a sweet-smelling pipe who likes to quote authors like they are personal friends, and I naively ask him what is the meaning of all this, why are we here, and he laughs a condescending academic laugh and says that even if he knew, he wouldn't tell me. And then I just go spinning out into airlessness, the planet earth a glowing ball millions of miles away.

I somehow manage to get on a plane and fly home. But of course, home is not a place to land– What's wrong with that Phyllis? There's always been something wrong with that girl! So I go back to Simmons and get through the rest of the year, studying harder, writing more papers. But academia, my one last hope, has abandoned me. The solace of ideas doesn't carry me anymore. I don't know how that rug was pulled out from under me, but it is gone.

If I can't be the good Jewish intellectual who marries the good Jewish doctor, well then, I had better DO "good." I volunteer for Vista in the South Bronx.

Chapter III

I t is 1967 now. I have come to help create a play street for inner city children, mostly Puerto Rican and a few Irish. My curly Jewish hair is even curlier in the steaming humidity of 152nd Street in the South Bronx. I am fresh out of that Boston intellectual nightmare where 19-year-old girls stretch their minds and their bodies across the Fenway and all over Harvard Square. But not me, me more like the monarch butterfly we had years later in a cardboard butterfly garden with plastic windows, the one that had one piece of its wing stuck to the cocoon. Couldn't fly off with the others and you couldn't help it either because if you so much as touch the fairy dust on its wings, its flight capacity is destroyed. Or so we were told.

And so she had to make her own way out of that cocoon which was itself flawed, and let's say for a moment that she did and that she went limping along the South Bronx tenement lined streets looking for that missing piece of her own wing in the rubble of broken windows and the smoggy tears of every crying child with outstretched hands pleading love me, see me, get me out of here. Looking for the lost pieces of herself in the urine-filled hallways and in all the distended bellies of all the rotting households finally cracked open, the juice of young lives spilled on the floor for the rats and cockroaches to mark with their tracks.

It is some kind of special garbage pickup day and literally, there are mountains of black plastic trash bags falling all over themselves into the stinking gutters. She is coming toward one such pile from this side and he is coming from that side and they both hear it at the same time, the faintest chirping of a tiny bird. Miraculously, he finds it and holds it in his hand. God only knows where its nest might have been. But Jimmy saves it and holds its little flightless wings in his artist hands and she loves him instantly. Not that way, but loves him as if he had plucked her very own self out of the trash crusher coming up the street.

Jimmy is a junkie. There is a story of a stepfather and a mother who tried to feed him scrambled eggs one day but the stepfather throws him out, doesn't want him eating their food. She talks about art with him. He shows her a sailboat he has made out of Popsicle sticks found on the street. It sits in waterless majesty on a table in his kitchen in an apartment that is grey and empty but perhaps for that table, a broken chair, and a mattress on the floor. She knows she is in danger being alone with him but she wants to save him as he saved the bird. She wants that so bad. She knows his artist soul as she knows her own, buried under mountains of trash. She tries to lure him out with a new set of pastel crayons and a drawing pad, tells him life is really worth living, even convinces him to go to rehab and he does. But not a few days later he is back on the street, had a fight there and they threw him out, and he is swallowed up again in heroin, swallowed up and spat out again each morning into the river of junkie puke that trickles down the sidewalk early, before the rest of the tenement hive is awake. She will see Jimmy one more time. I imagine he is now long since swallowed up for good. They all were, even little Juan, the 13 year old in the patched together family she lived with that summer. Dead from heroin.

Marco is another Vista Volunteer, a recovering black heroin addict who is probably long dead by now, too. I turn into him like a car turning into a dead end street. Make it night, make it smell like alcohol; make it a car full of drunk men careening down a NYC boulevard. I scream until they let us out.

I don't know where we are. All I know is, I have to get myself *out* of the car. But it isn't over. Initiation by Fire in a flea-bitten hotel in Harlem. Make it somewhere that makes your skin crawl but your legs and your guts are frozen and can't take you home because there is no home, not inside or out. The fluorescent light in the kitchen in Plainfield is still humming and the avocado green dish drain is still clean by the sink far away. But no, just swallow the last bit of your voice that cried to get out of the car, swallow it now, and let his tongue in.

Where am I? I'm right here where I've been all along. *This* is where I have been, in some cyclone chaos of sex and death and screams that die inside lips cemented shut. *I know this place so well.*

Marco actually is quite kind to her, if you can say having sex with a paralyzed girl is kind. Perhaps in his own lost way, he feels some twisted kinship with her, and she, of course, feels that with him. Twisted kinship as in, I am drawn to you like dust into a vacuum cleaner, the remaining specks of me sucked into your sad-eyed emptiness to make some illusory room clean while in fact I live here mute in a dark accumulation of shame. So it's not as if she tries to fight him off; she doesn't. She is *way* too far gone for that. She is just grateful he thinks to wash her off when it's over. Walking out of the subway the next day past

39

a fruit market and mothers pushing strollers and yelling for their bigger children to catch up, walking with a certain discomfort in the blinding smear of sunlight, she wonders if she is still a virgin. She really isn't sure.

But there was this moment, just a few days before, when they were sitting together in the grass at the edge of a big New York City parkway. They talked, he a black boy from the projects with no education, ties to the Mafia he said, and sad eyes filled with longing for her, *perhaps* for her or perhaps only for the imaginary elixir of life, a white virgin cocktail. She on her way to have lunch with her father who had come into the city to see her, lunch at some very fancy Italian restaurant where he and her mother had dined and raved about the food, where you didn't order but were served one dish after another until you couldn't eat another bite. And the desserts, oi, you've never seen such desserts.

She on her way to lunch with her father. Black boy with sweat on his soft upper lip under the sparse black bristle of his underdeveloped beard. Soft lips, sad eyes, sweat, longing for her. Clean-shaven father in a pressed suit, a normal American father on his way to lunch with his socially conscious Vista Volunteer daughter. Two worlds almost colliding, so close as their orbits approach that for one spilt second she can see the sun sparkling off the well-swept steps leading up to the back door of the house on West Eighth Street, so close she can smell brisket in the oven. Two planets this close to colliding, but *her* world flies past in an orbit all its own. Her world is Marco's world, gaseous, uninhabitable, and dark like the basement of the moon. What part of consciousness sees these two worlds screaming to within inches of each other and then hurls the unwary space traveler out into airless midnight skies, feeling the discrepancies like razors on baby flesh and yet feeling nothing at all? What part of consciousness looks blankly into the imminent crater of an impact of that magnitude and then pleasantly eats a big Italian lunch?

Well, there was no going back to Simmons after that, no going back to dress codes and curfews, smoking lounges and floor monitors. I move to NYC, enroll in the New School College. I call John from my apartment in Brooklyn. I know from my brother that he is in NYC visiting his mother. Of course, he comes over.

Maybe there is a way back to Eden, to before the Fall. He is the only good boyfriend of all the ones I ever had, not that I actually had "boyfriends." Maybe if I can find a way to let John in, I can be good again, wash all the badness away. But I'm like Alice– I've drunk something from a vial and I can't fit through the door to John, or he to me.

He actually asks me if he can touch my breasts. You don't know where I've been, John. And I don't tell him. "I'm sorry. I'm so sorry. I just can't." And he goes away for the last time, sweetly, kindly, as before. And I am sitting on my bed, praying to God to make me good.

To make me good? Oh, Eve, is that what you had to do? All those years out of Eden – pray to God to make you good, take you back? Kept forever from simply embracing and loving the good man who was yours because of some supposed evil between men and women you were never allowed to know or understand?

I've never prayed before, but I am sitting on my bed crying and praying to God to make me good, to love me.

*Well, let me tell you, if you pray to a God that has to make you good, that's the kind of God you will get, one who just can't wait to tell you exactly what you have to do to BE good in his eyes, to be loved by him. You don't get the God who says, "But sweetheart, you ARE good. You are loved just the way you are." And you don't get the God who whispers to you through the grass, who holds you in a hot wind embrace and washes your parched feet with water. And yet sometimes that God appears anyway. I had forgotten all about **that God, the one** who found me in Boston Commons. But mercifully, that God returned.*

Chapter IV

I t happens for me the first night I arrive in Arizona. In a crack in time, I end up in the Mojave Desert. It is the summer of 1968. My brother's girlfriend at Radcliffe gets me a volunteer position in Harvard's American Indian Project. I am on the bus coming up to Kingman from Phoenix. Never felt a heat like that before, heavy, breathless, drawing the moisture out of your lungs like salt on a slug. But now that heat has fallen over the horizon and she sleeps peacefully as the bus takes her out into the desert. She wakes up to a sky you never see in New Jersey or Boston, a sky that opens into forever. And the moon opens her door into a black velvet garden spilling over with starflowers, silver light petals falling all the way to the desert floor in a soft dry rain, drenching the warm sand in reverse silhouettes.

The claustrophobic walls of the tiny Brooklyn apartment she came from open out into a whole planet's worth of sky. It's this sky more than anything else that takes her — not gently by the hand or securely by the waist like a long awaited hero might take the fair maiden to safety — no, the desert sky takes her out of everything she thought she knew about herself.

I am suddenly not the center of my universe.

In a moment, the East Coast Phyllis who held onto life by a fraying thread, whose little spirit went out the window anyway, that same Phyllis suddenly finds herself in the right proportion to life, as a grain of sand knows itself in proportion to the sea and gives itself to the waves.

There must have been a Home once because I have returned. *I'm Home.*

I have come to work with off-reservation Walapai Indian children in a government-funded summer recreation program. Driving down a lazy street in Kingman, I see them for the first time, the Walapais, with their beautiful dark skin and black hair. I look at them and I want to dive into the round pool of a brown face and swim there all the way Home to that place where I once walked in moccasins over these same rocks. But I am brought up achingly short by my own reflection—the white skin, the Semitic nose and the thick frizzy hair. How did this happen? Why am I in this white body and this white mind? They won't recognize me! She looks longingly from the car window at the brown and white store-made moccasins on flat wide feet and she resolves to buy a pair and wear them.

Nevertheless, this Mohave summer is ecstasy. It is everything deserts are not supposed to be. It is food, it is water, and it is cool balm on all the burnt places I have hidden behind well-written papers and excellent grades.

*Mother Earth picks me up and holds me in her lap and speaks to me the way a mother should. She tells me her secrets and sings through my hair like the wind in the cactus needles. And I can almost feel breasts under my dress. I can almost feel hips and the places that make pollen. I don't have to please Mother Earth; I don't have to be **good** for her. I am her daughter: she **wants** to love me. She speaks to me everywhere. She speaks to me through the creases in the hills and the broken skeletons of long ago cactus and I, human being, am no different from them. She tells me about gravity and how the principles*

44

of the earth's functioning are exactly the same as those governing the human psyche. I don't think to write anything down. We are just talking, the earth and I, everywhere I go. And for the very first time I am not lonely.

I am a speck of sand and a speck in time. There are moments when I am more dry thistle than I am the Jewish girl with curly hair having a Harvard American Indian Project experience. There are moments when I am more rock than flesh, more wind than breath.

This is how I find myself in the desert, a seed left over from some prehistoric time, breathing only the faintest of unhurried breaths until this moment when the smell of rain, traveling from miles and lifetimes away, comes inevitably toward me on the next wind.

But it's the late sixties and no one I know talks about this kind of God. They are all talking meditation and the astral plane and India and karma, so I have no language for this Mother Earth. And the one person I meet out here in the desert who does speak this language is a married man, an artist named Tim, and I go with him where I always seem to go.

It's my last night now. Tomorrow I fly back to NYC and my last year of college. I want to stay. I want to stay so bad. I picture myself in a little house on the edge of town, a desert hermit, needing no one, needing nothing but this dry ground. I go up to my favorite rock after dark to say goodbye to the Mohave, or not to say goodbye but to make the last moment last just a little longer. I'm waiting for Tim but I go early to have time alone. I tell God I want to stay here and I ask deep inside myself for permission. The answer is immediate and clear. "No," is the answer, "No, Phyllis, you have already had lifetimes like this. You have to go back and work it out with people." It's not a loving voice and it's not unloving either. It is just the truth and I don't even know how I know that. I don't know who is speaking, but I don't question it. Neither do I ask exactly what it means.

And so I go back to NYC, right back into the waiting arms of that God who can't wait to tell me how to be good. How quickly I lose Goddess Mother Earth. I can't have Her now. I have some other work to do, but I don't know what it is. I wake up back inside the tight white skin of a lonely seeker on a concrete highway somewhere in Brooklyn. I'm dead meat for Mr. N who is the leader of the Gurdjieff group. Though Mr. N does have something to offer, he is also a very 60's wolf in sheep's clothing, a very striking, well-spoken old man with white hair and blue eyes playing God to a group of earnest spiritual devotees in bell-bottoms and braids.

Chapter V

I move up to Warwick, NY to join the group. Mr. N was with Gurdjieff in Paris and he's teaching us how to Work on ourselves, to "wake up" in a spiritual sense. We're supposed to create an impartial observer that gathers information about our unconsciousness, but what impartiality can a 21-year-old girl create to a corpse of herself lying in the back of her own throat? Still, I do try to work on myself. I do try to be good for this God with the piercing blue eyes and a Scandinavian accent.

Actually, he seems quite down to earth; he understands people like me. He speaks right into my heart; he *sees* me. We're growing a big group garden and cooking meals together and he's teaching us Movements, ancient sacred dances that Gurdjieff discovered in remote temples of Eastern Russia. And you can go and talk with Mr. N. You just ask for an appointment. Well, he doesn't always see everybody, but he sees me, most of the time.

He takes the group on a trip across country to visit all the cities where he has established other Gurdjieff groups, holding meetings, setting the stage, I imagine, for all possible "friction" with ourselves and other people as I understood Gurdjieff did in Paris—to wake us up out of our deep sleep of unconsciousness. That's what this work on ourselves is all about.

My parents, of course, don't know what to make of me at all, as I slip farther and farther from their known world, but they kindly buy me a beautiful powder blue down sleeping bag for the trip. I am in it now, under the trees in Arkansas or somewhere hot and humid where a down sleeping bag is not actually the best protection from the mosquitos, but it's all I have. I wake up in the middle of the night, *not the kind of waking up* Mr. N is talking about. I wake up and I am out of my body. I see three very tall men in black standing over me. Terror like you cannot imagine. I have to get back into my body or I know I will die. There is a scream I have to scream but I can't find my mouth. I can't find it! I have to get back inside and scream! And then suddenly I am back in my body and the men are gone and I don't have the scream but I don't care. I'm back. That's all that matters.

We're back in Warwick now and my parents come to visit. Mr. N invites us all into his office. Maybe he's telling my parents I'm a good girl, you know, succeeding at whatever it is I'm doing there, which would be like talking Greek to my parents anyway because there is no imaginable "success" in their minds for a daughter who is "finding herself" in a run-down old Barn full of Hippies in tie-dyed home-made clothes. Come on! Who are we fooling? But they are polite. They're probably looking for any sign of respectability here, and Mr. N, after all, holds a number of Ph.Ds.

When we leave, Mr. N follows us down the hallway back into the main part of the Barn, and just as my parents go around a corner, he pulls me to him and gives me a big wet kiss, just a split second away from where my parents might have turned and caught a horrifying glimpse. But they don't. I'm scared and embarrassed and I am happy. He loves me. I'm good enough.

He kisses me around the corner from his old wife, too, and I know *she sees*.

*God cast Eve out of Eden, but he felt her up right outside Eden's back door. Then he had the nerve to blame it all on the Serpent and on Eve herself. Why couldn't God just be happy to BE flesh in the first place? Why did he have to pretend he was above all that? And why did I have to wander around trying to earn his love back? You should have been home with your wife, Mr. N. You should have kissed her grey hair and held her old bones, you know, the bones that carried **your** two children. You should have kept your hands to yourself.*

But I'm so chosen. I REALLY don't see, and I don't say anything.

*I wonder if Eve talked after Eden. I wonder if she told anyone what happened or was she, too, silenced by a shame that was not hers? Did you figure it out, Eve? That you and Adam HAD to leave that so-called Eden, not because you were bad but because it was run by a **False God**? One who blamed you for being in the very body he gave you! One who needed to withhold the knowledge you craved so he could keep his power over you! One who wanted you begging for forgiveness for what HE did to you! You were too smart for that, weren't you, Eve?*

I wasn't.

Chapter VI

I was given the job of running the Guest House where people coming up from New York City could stay to attend workdays at the Barn. Running the Guest House was the perfect job for me. It gave me a purpose and a sense of belonging, however shaky and inauthentic it might have been. The illusory sense of control it brought me—I could make sure everyone got up on time just the way my father did when I was a kid. I could make sure all the dishes were washed and put away, albeit we had to heat water in a kettle and the splintering wooden floor could never be washed clean. The Guest House might have been a hotel once but by the time the group found it, it was a dirty, dilapidated, unheated, abandoned building, like many of the houses in Warwick at the time. But it was the Hippie era and doing without the comforts of civilization was considered a value back then. We were all outcasts of the fifties in one way or another, some of us a bit more outcast than others. But we were sincerely trying to find value in something other than a bank account and new furniture.

I wanted to keep Mr. N's love so badly, but he moved on to another girl who was agonizingly earnest and had much bigger breasts. I knew how to be cast out.

But I found Bill: Moth to Flame. Bill is a wild man. Five and a half years younger than me, he roars around in a huge beater of an old red truck that he later tells me has a hole in the floor he pees into (through a hose) to save time. Well, I guess he thinks I'm really something—maybe it's nothing more than that I am in charge of the Guest House. Maybe it looks like I know something, that I have something to offer. Whatever it is, I take it for love.

It's 1974. I'm 27 and pregnant. I've left the Guest House and we're living together in an old apartment in Florida, NY. Bill is on the phone talking about a construction job. He's had too much to drink, more than I realize I guess, because his tongue is thick and his words are slurred. He drinks a lot of beer, but this is something new.

I have a baby inside me. I KNOW I should not marry Bill. I know this is a huge mistake. But *I choose* to bury that knowing. There is simply no way I'm having a baby alone and *of course,* I'm having this baby. So I marry Bill. We plan our wedding for December 22, the darkest, shortest day of the year.

We look for God everywhere but in each other.

I've married a man who drinks way too much. He seems to hate everything he was ever attracted to in me and he is addicted to his search for God more than he is addicted to alcohol even.

...Seven years later, nothing has changed. I walk around in my little house in the woods, pregnant with our third child, making my own yogurt and teaching first grade in the Gurdjieff group's parent-run school. Bill meditates for hours behind a closed bedroom door, and I wonder what is wrong with me.

"I'm getting to Nirvana this life, and you're not going to stop me." He actually said that. I'm not sure I had an answer. But you know, all those words you don't say never disappear. They just go on boiling like an unattended kettle, until its screech becomes a scream you cannot NOT hear. I felt it first in the summer of 1984, way down deep in my stomach. It wanted to come up through my throat and out of my mouth, but I *didn't* want it to in the worst way. I *can't* hear it, I *won't*, I *can't*. But it waits for me patiently, like a lion asleep in the sun by my front door.

Chapter VII

We are all so hot to please the latest version of God. Meditation is the rage. Mr. N has died and a lot of our Gurdjieff group has moved on to Swami Muktananda and Siddha Yoga and incense and chanting. Bill has moved on with them, me hanging around the fringes so as not to be completely left out.

We're walking into the Satsang one night and Lois is coming up to the door from another direction. As I watch her, a pang shoots through my very pregnant body—She's the Other Woman!

Bill and Lois have been practicing music together for the Satsang for several months now. They're jogging together in the early mornings. I am uneasy but I try to let it go—until I can't manage that anymore.

"Are you having an affair?" I ask him. "It *feels* like an affair."

He looks at me in disgust. "What's wrong with you that you can't let me have a woman for a friend?"

Silence. What *is* wrong with me?

I have the baby, Daniel. Excruciating home birth. 9 pounds 2 ounces. Body feels like it is tearing apart. Bill's parents are in the living room, watching our two other children, Eddie and Izzi.

Much later, they go back to their hotel and we try to sleep. I wake up in a puddle of blood. I ask Bill to help me. I need to go to the bathroom and there is blood everywhere.

He tells me to go to Hell and goes back to sleep.

I am IN HELL. That old God didn't have to condemn me to anything more than this. Hell is right here in this wasteland outside the door of Love.

Eventually I tell Bill to get out and he goes, to Lois's I guess. I want to die.

"You create your own reality." That one phrase from the Siddha Yoga Correspondence Course leaves me suicidal, as if I wasn't already. If I created *this reality*, well– I really would rather be dead. But maybe it's true… The old God still has me.

Can't sleep, can barely eat, nursing a baby, agonizing anxiety running through my breasts where sweet milk should be. Poor Daniel. That's all I have, little baby. Then one night Bill slips back into my bed and we pick up the shreds of ourselves. Nothing is said. Nothing. I am too undone to move. I tell myself maybe he is sorry. Maybe we can put something back together — well, not really. I tell myself nothing. I already know how to hold on by a thread. It's nothing new.

Chapter VIII

C hris is a very kind man from the Gurdjieff group who has become an avid devotee of Muktananda. He is all about the mala beads, how many hours he meditates, and the pure bliss streaming into his Third Eye. He surely radiates happiness. One day he shares with me his ecstasy about taking a Sanskrit class at the Ashram. But as he talks, I hear something he *isn't* saying. I hear, "Love me, God. Please love me! I'll do anything. I'll learn Sanskrit, I'll meditate and chant 100 hours a week if you will just love me, God!"

Most likely, I am seeing *myself* in him. But the point is, I see MYSELF. I see that underneath all my spiritual striving is the very same need to be loved that has always been there. And I know then that I want to be loved *by people*, that God has become my default lover and it isn't working. I can't find a way to please that God enough for him to STAY, to *show me the way in the world*. Even the most beautiful flashes of light every few years don't cut it. I want a love that is accessible to me, Phyllis. I want love in the world of people. I want to love myself. I don't want a husband who was looking for God. I want a husband who was looking for *me*. I want someone to help me get the kids to school, do a few dishes, hold me, and light up when I come into the room.

In that moment, *I stopped looking for God altogether*. There had to be something I could figure out about why love had been so elusive. There had to be something I could heal.

I went to therapy. I went just long enough to discover that your childhood has a definite impact on the rest of your life. That was complete news to me. I told the therapist I had a good childhood, that my parents loved me. The problems, I said, were in my marriage. And so Bill and I went to therapy together and actually, it was good for a while. It really was. We talked. There was a lot that wasn't said, but it was a start. Then the issue of Bill's drinking came up and after that, it all unraveled.

When you can't face the dragon, you run, even if you call it something else. So, following another of Bill's dreams of liberation, we sold our house and uprooted ourselves from our community in NY. We had no plan beyond spending the summer at the X Institute where yet again, Bill hoped (and I convinced myself I agreed) to find release from our insanity in someone else's "healing" modality. We spent I don't know how many thousands of dollars from the sale of our house to camp out in a tent on their property with our kids and go through yet another faulty gauntlet.

I can't blame Bill for that. I didn't say no. I wanted to. I knew what we were doing was crazy, but I didn't say no. I tried to make myself believe we were going on a huge adventure most people wouldn't dare undertake, a modern day vision quest perhaps. But the truth was we had no vision. And *I knew better*. I knew I should have left Bill in NY. Everything in me knew better than to do this but I couldn't face being alone with three children. I couldn't face being alone period. And so we sold our house and ran.

I don't know what I thought I was going to get out of that summer. I don't know what innovative exercises I thought I could do that would fix my marriage, make me happy, or take me off the edge of that cliff I was always standing on. I had absolutely no concept that healing meant opening up a wound and cleaning it out. I was still trying to figure out how to be good, do it *right*, get that kind of A. But despite myself, the wound opened.

In a guided visualization one day, I had a powerful vision of myself lying on my back with my head arched back and a Scream coming out of my mouth…

Mid-way through the summer, Bill tells me he wants to "explore his sexuality" with a woman at the X Institute. Two of the participants are already openly having an affair and I guess that is all the permission Bill thinks he needs.

I don't know where I find this part of myself, but I actually tell him he can go ahead and explore all he wants -- I just won't be there when he's done. I think he's shocked. He doesn't "explore" after all. And that lethal bond I have with him is finally broken. *I don't love Bill.* All these years aching for him to love me have come to this. *I* don't love *him*. And I know now it is only a matter of time.

And still I don't leave. I know I should. I'm offered a job at the school where my kids have been in summer camp. I'm sure I can find a place to live in this beautiful little New England town. Many people seem to like me here. I could start again alone. But I don't take the job. All I knew is that I have to get back to the Southwest. I have to find that girl with braids and moccasins in the desert. I have to go Home.

We buy a van and set out for Arizona.

Chapter IX

W e've been out on the road for weeks now, pretending to be a family on vacation but really, we are $32,000 away from homelessness. We are camped on a beach at Lake Havasu, on the barren artificiality of a lake that has no business being there, just as *we* have no business being there. It's the middle of the night. I wake up and I can't breathe, can't think, blood rushing through me like a flash flood, tearing up the last foundations of "home" and washing them away. I'm going to die if I don't get myself into a house. I know this. Bill doesn't want to know.

Somehow, we make it to Kingman and rent a small duplex on Wickiup Street. But I can't find that old wind, I can't hear her song. There is no young girl-woman in braids waiting for me around the next outcropping of rock. I am not called to any open skyline but sucked instead down a narrow dark passage inside myself. We put the kids in school and day care and I sit in a tiny bare kitchen day after day, writing and writing and writing. That's all I know how to do.

One thing emerges and one thing only. It comes like a shark attack, seemingly out of nowhere—I was abducted. *I wrote that*, but I don't know who is holding my pen. *I was abducted*–the words bite into me and will not let go. I try to fight them off with my conscious mind. It says No, I would remember. But my conscious mind is no match for these teeth. My *body* says Yes, *I* remember, here, in the back of my throat and in the teeth biting through my lips... The man in the car.... No, it can't be. I would remember...

There is a whole other God out there who has a whole other face. This God has only one requirement, and that is that you LISTEN, and even that is not really a requirement. It is a choice. This God waits patiently, waits forever if need be, for you to choose to hear what is already being spoken, what you already know. This one does not speak from a mountaintop. This God lives and speaks inside you. And this God spoke to Phyllis in a deserted little kitchen in the desert– the desert, where seekers have gone for thousands of years to find God. I wonder if Eve found her God in the desert outside of Eden. Of course, Phyllis didn't recognize this face as God, but she's a writer. She couldn't stop writing and in writing, she had opened the door to this God. After that, it would not close again.

I got what I came back to the desert for, and it wasn't refuge and it wasn't that big sky after all. The same voice that told me I couldn't stay there 17 years before — well, that God meant it — that door was closed, that window shut, and I *had* to go "back" and figure out what it meant to "work it out with people."

I knew what I had to do. I had started graduate school in Social Work before we left NY. I was going back to school. We had friends in Santa Fe, NM who we had visited on our way to Arizona. I had wanted to stay. Santa Fe felt good to me, but staying meant that Bill would have to go back to work, the fantasy of our vision-quest/delusional thinking would have to end, and he wasn't ready and I didn't argue because I was still holding out for Kingman. But after that voice spoke again, the real vision inherent in our faulty quest was clear, and it wasn't any kind of life baking out in the graveled yard of an empty little duplex on Wickiup Street. I was going back to school, I was going to make my own life, and Bill could come or not. I don't know if he really wanted to follow *me*, but he came. Maybe he didn't know what else to do.

Two years later, we are living in a shabby little rental in Santa Fe with discolored shag carpeting and goat-heads in the back yard. But I made it. I'm in graduate school in Psychology. I will get a degree. I will make my own living.

It's morning and I'm alone. I am in the shower. The Scream is in my throat, right behind my tongue. It's palpable; as if a fully formed being is there inside me saying, I'm here, listen to me. And I simply say okay. Okay. And then it starts– huge racking sobs, screams and screams and screams and then, out of *my throat* comes the wailing of a newborn baby. I hear it. I hear her. I hear her crying and I know *whatever it was, it started long before abduction; it started way back at beginning.*

I'm learning about family dynamics in my graduate program. I'm in a hypnosis class. I do my internship in a sexual abuse treatment program. *I'm remembering.* I *see* that baby in the bassinette. I *feel* the pain in the back of her throat. And the scream turns into a voice. It says NO to Bill, NO to the alcohol and drugs, and NO to whatever God he still worships. It says, **No More**. No more abuse.

*Did Eve turn around in the Wilderness and scream NO to that God in the Garden? Did she tell him she **remembers** now and she isn't taking the blame anymore, she isn't going to slink out of the garden like a criminal with her lips sealed? Did she tell him she found another God all by herself, a God who talks to her and tells her the truth? I hope she did.*

We get divorced.

And still there is no relief. In my new reality of homework, bills, and three kids by myself, I am holding onto a hot pad and my sanity by the barest of threads for a long, long time, years, while waves of remembering wash over me.

***

Four years later, I am flying to Massachusetts alone, meeting up with my children who have been with Bill and his family. It is the summer of 1991. There is a terrible lightning storm all up and down the east coast and we cannot land anywhere. The plane is circling, buffeted by horrible winds. I'm clutching the arms of my seat and in my mind's eye, I spiral into death in a plane crash. At some point, I realize I'm not in my body, that oddly enough, I am outside the window of the plane in some psychic way and I need to get back into my body. I have this overwhelming feeling that I will actually be okay, no matter what the turbulence, if I can just get back into my body.

I see the infant again. I go out the window, leave my little body lying on the bassinette while I hover outside on the sill. I don't leave completely and I don't come back in either.

I can't tell you how I know, I just do. A part of my life force left my body and never came all the way back. It left through that infant's cry and it hovered outside the window. I have been somewhere halfway between life and death since then in a way I can't explain, even to myself. I just *know*, and in the knowing I return to my seat in the airplane and I breathe now, years of breath back into my body, and all my panic subsides.

Living in The Garden of Eden is living safe inside your own body. You knew that, Eve. That's why you left.

The following year I take my two sons to Canyonlands in Utah. I can't seem to get back to the desert the way I need to, even though I live in the desert now. I'm looking for something there and I keep going back for it without knowing what it is. We are in a campground outside Monument Valley on our way home and it doesn't get more down to bedrock than this. The boys are off climbing and I am sitting in the sun with my journal. Two pictures of Phyllis stand side by side in my mind. One is Phyllis in the Arizona desert in 1968, the girl with braids and a flowered dress, who had a love affair with the open sky and was kissed by mother earth and sung to by the wind. The other is the Phyllis who has been climbing out of the bowels of the earth for eons, who has nightmares of being chased by men with knives, who still gasps when someone comes up suddenly behind her, who is studying psychology, going to therapy, and looking for love with a man. Do I ever come together or do I travel this whole life split like two parallel lines?

On the way home, I have another one of those moments. I have to stop the car somewhere right near the NM border, nothing but desert everywhere, a black mesa off in the distance. I hear Mother Earth calling me and I get out of the car and sit by the side of the road.

*I hear her, I feel her take me bodily again in her arms, my Mother the Earth. She comes for me again. She comes **into my body** and weeps with me with the joy of our union. **That's what a loving God does—it comes for you.** It weeps with you AND it fills you with love.*

*Mother Earth was the **only one** who made it safe for me to be in my body. My body and the body of the Earth, together. Who would have ever guessed?*

I can't imagine what my children thought of me sitting there sobbing in the dust. There was nothing I could do about it anyway. She came for me.

I think she was preparing me for my last descent.

PART III—God Came Looking For Me

Chapter I

Y ou know what magnets are like, how powerful the pull is in one direction, and how strong the resistance is in the other? Sometimes it's like that in real life — you are either drawn powerfully to someone or something or you are repulsed. But some magnetism is much more subtle or concealed. You are drawn to just where you need to go without ever realizing it until much later.

I could have done the required internship for my Masters Degree at any one of a number of agencies, worked with any number of client populations, but I was drawn straight into a sexual abuse treatment program that focused on child victims and their families, as well as adult survivors and perpetrators. I read book after book on incest and sexual abuse and I saw something of myself in every story. I wrote my Master's Thesis on the hypothesis that people who are sexually abused as children are more likely than others to be abused again as adults, that their inner radar and protective mechanisms are impaired early on making them easier prey. I read Alice Miller's books from cover to cover as you might read a juicy novel.

My parents asked to read my Thesis and I let them. My father corrected all the grammatical mistakes and said nothing. My mother's only comment was, "Don't you think some of that is normal? Like little boys putting sticks up you?" My mother was the first girl after six boys.

No matter how much I read, I couldn't get enough, and yet, at the very same time, I couldn't get it at all. And I *didn't want* to get it. It might be like researching all your symptoms and they all point to cancer. You really want to know what's wrong with you, you really want to get better, but you don't want THAT diagnosis. You don't want THAT kind of treatment. Maybe you're just making too much out of those symptoms anyway. Maybe you're a hypochondriac, maybe you're nuts. Maybe if you had been a better person, you would have created a better reality. You would have had a loving husband. Your kids wouldn't be suffering and you wouldn't be so damned depressed. You'd smile and laugh more and you'd stop being obsessed with yourself. Quit talking about PAIN already!

I went to a number of therapists after I left Bill and I tried so hard to make sense of myself with them. But the mind is a very curious thing. Once it gets hold of a picture or a belief, it seems like it just won't let go. My mind had taken me so far away from what actually happened to me that it simply refused to come back. It wouldn't let go of the belief that the problem was me. I wrote out all my symptoms, read them again and again, trying to convince myself there really was no room for doubt, like a lawyer in a courtroom might present his case. "There is just overwhelming evidence, Your Honor." And still I was overwhelmed with doubt. The first time a therapist suggested that the terrifying images in my head might be related to *real* events, that they were not aberrations of a disturbed mind, I was in shock. I was that far away from believing anything rearing up from my unconscious, no matter how repetitive the messages were.

Finally, my psyche simply said Okay, let's try again. In 1993, I found someone who could be there while I went all the way down to that underworld, who held the lifeline while I dove back under and retrieved the girl *who did get into the car after all.* It was a treacherous journey. While I craved those sessions, once there I just didn't want those memories to be mine.

I kept a journal of everything I was uncovering in case I ever managed to get out alive and had something to share with others. Maybe I would be able to shine a little light on that dark road I had travelled so long alone – that is, *if* I could ever reach the light.

You could say I was looking for "healing," for an end to the gripping pain in my throat and chest. I just wanted to be able to love and be loved by a man. That was what healing meant to me.

But that was not exactly the journey I was to make.

On December 10, 1994, I had a most remarkable experience. I was in a therapy session, working with very disturbing feelings of abuse when suddenly a delicate, rhythmic, otherworldly vibration of light pulsated in my forehead. Love and life-giving energy vibrated down my throat and into my heart. Golden light filled me. And then the vibration enveloped me from the outside, rippling in huge waves around my entire body. I heard this message, *"There is a God. This is God and this is how you know God."* This same voice said, *"Surrender totally. Surrender everything– your pain, your practice, your children, your preconceptions of how things should be and what should happen. Surrender your life. Give it to God."* Golden light shone down from a point inside the top of my head. Then *"Nothing is yours. This is how you find happiness. I'm showing you the Way. In this moment, it is golden and completely unobstructed. You will carve the Way out of the stones and dirt of real life experience. It will not always look golden, but remember this. Don't ever look at life the same way again. Make surrender your practice."*

And so God came to me once again *through my body*, found me in the very body I so desperately avoided feeling and yet struggled so hard to love all my life. This was not my Mother Earth God. This was a whole new God, an even bigger God if that makes any sense.

Even so, panic, anxiety, and despair took over once again and dominated both my days and my nights. By February of the following year, I was at rock bottom. In therapy, I *saw* the man in the car. I saw his face. I knew I had gotten in. But the release of these most terrible memories seemed to offer me no relief. I was stuck in a no-man's land of doubting every memory, even with body sensations and emotions I knew I could not have made up. At the very same time, I wanted desperately to be believed. The memories just explained too much of my life. They solved the riddle of the jagged pieces of a puzzle I had never been able to put together. And while that was undeniably true, I felt insane with relentless doubt. My family looked so normal. *And I wasn't getting better.*

Meanwhile, my journal was my place of refuge. It was where I went when there was nowhere else to go. And so, once again, I wrote and wrote and wrote. I had no idea of the miraculous journey that was about to unfold through those pages. What follows is taken from of the journal I kept.

***

In February of 1995, I wrote,

What if I trusted it all, no matter how bizarre? The things I see in my head while someone's body–mine–is shaking and crying don't fit anything I know. But I cannot deny the shaking, the crying, and the cold that comes over me and makes my teeth chatter. Every spiritual path I've taken, every therapy, every moment of light or insight or opening always takes me back to this place. Now it seems so obvious. I'm not crazy. I've said I'm crazy and I've said I'm making it up and I've hated myself and I've shut up the cry and I've doubted and I've wanted to protect my parents and I've preferred to believe that my childhood was the way I remembered it. And at the same time, I've been dying inside just as much from doubting as from what happened to me. So, it's all or nothing. I know that in my soul. It all has the same quality of being true. I have to swallow it all. I have to live to discover what this all means. I have to have my whole truth. I want to live my whole truth.

I see how I go outside my body and disconnect. So today, I am trying with all my might to stay inside my body and feel it from inside and stop the denying voices and the judgments. I'm so sorry. I went out and bought Sad Eyed Lady of the Lowlands and I cried my eyes out listening to it. I remember my*self* in this song.

I have the most bizarre image of a room with a black cloth pinned over the window. There is a man on my left with instruments; he is doing some kind of medical procedure. But it isn't a doctor's office. I feel like I am being tortured. And as I see this, I keep saying I'm crazy over and over again. Yet it comes, like everything else, like a pang in my chest. It is *told* inside me. I want to deny it. I don't want to tell this to anyone. It's the man in the car. It's wherever he took me.

There is an inescapable and relentless conversation between my rational mind and this source of information that does not come through my mind. Back and forth, back and forth in endless fruitless argument with myself, landing nowhere.

I think I can finally feel love for that lonely one in me and I'm sad for her that she suffered so long alone. I don't want to run from these feelings anymore. I cannot give her the message that her pain is too much for me. I cannot run from her like my family still does. She holds my soul. She is wrapped around it like a child holding on for dear life in the dark. She has never let go. She has called to me for years and I didn't know what I heard. But I have held onto her just as fiercely as I pushed her away because I knew I needed her, I knew she was the key. She is wrapped around my soul and if I want to have my soul back whole, she comes with it. *It all comes down to total acceptance of all her pain.*

And still, there is a part of me that, no matter what, *refuses* to believe that anything happened. I talk to it like I am talking to another person, reminding it of all my symptoms, but the voices are dim and the memory of what I am telling myself comes without any emotion of recognition, as if I am quoting lines out of a book about someone else's life. So today, I found myself having this conversation again and it is as if I am trying to convince the un-convincible, reciting a long list of facts to a blank wall. But this time I stopped and asked myself who is this part that just doesn't know and can't be convinced and doesn't hear and doesn't feel? And for the first time I'm thinking, perhaps this "non-self" is *the one who got me through*. I'm sure she was, now that I say it. So I can't be hard on her because she was the best friend to me that she knew how to be. At the same time, I just have to find a way to bring these two parts back together. I have to honor that the force behind her absolutely not knowing *anything* had to have been tremendous.

I see myself write these words and I start into the floating dream space again. And the conversation, that same old conversation is still going on inside my head but it has moved out of the range of my hearing.

Help me put these two parts together, God.

I'm having endless anxiety and panic attacks, the desire to hurt myself, feelings of something terrible about to happen or already happened, the feeling of being totally disconnected from physical reality and disconnected from all love and from the human race, and the feeling of wishing I were dead, total hopelessness and overwhelming pain, and absolute inability to leave my house or be with other people. I'm back to hanging on by a thread. Help me God, to submit on a deeper level and not lose faith so easily.

...Went on a hike with my son Eddie this afternoon. It was nice to be with him outside and feel safe. But as soon as we started driving home, I could feel the desperation and the anxiety come up again. I was okay as long as I could tell myself I was having panic for a reason. I'm not crazy. Then this huge force of doubt came over me and I felt like I was going over some irreversible edge. Eddie went off to be with friends. I sat on my bed, unable to do anything but talk to this crying one inside. I told her that I loved her. I told her I was willing to hear whatever she has to say about the panic.

I sat down with my journal and this is what I wrote:

Dear sweet sad-eyed girl, I know how terrified you were to turn inside, how there was almost no place of safety or comfort in there. And at the same time, I know how desperately you tried to go inside anyway because you knew that your heart and your soul were in there and if you were to ever find relief or a connection to God, you had to be able to get inside. You couldn't touch your soul without awakening all the pain. And I have to accept that one brings the other. I keep being called back so that I don't leave something buried that needs to be unearthed. It's not because I am a crazy misfit. She doesn't want me to be afraid of her.

And then quite out of nowhere, this Voice began to speak to me and write in my journal through my own hand.

We love you. Thank you for giving Us this opening today. We are showing you that your soul and your truth are one and the same. For now. We are telling you to not be afraid. You have NOTHING TO LOSE from trusting, NOTHING. This is Our word. This is from GOD. You have everything to lose from not trusting. You know the truth of that already. Not trusting is contracting the opening for your soul to a pinhole. Trusting is opening the door to heaven on earth. LET GO, SWEETHEART, FLY. LET GO. What We are saying is beyond surrender though surrender is a good word for you humans. You do not want this to be a narrow, constricted, tortured path any more than it has to be. WE will help you. If you feel fear, write to Her (the lost terrified one inside me) *as you did today. We are standing right behind Her. Isn't this the best proof We could give you? Write to her and you will find Us.*

You see now that she is nothing more than the particular shadow your soul chose to cast on this earth to draw you to it. Do you see now why there is nothing to fear, why it is pointless to resist? And again, that is all part of the learning. Not a mistake on your part that you didn't see this sooner. We are so glad you are here. You do not need to focus on the earthly situation. It has never been in your hands, none of it, ever. That is just an illusion human beings have to calm themselves. You need only focus on Her and We will hear that as a knocking on Our door. And you'll see. The door will open. We are ready to go now.

Once again, a veil is lifted. Once again, there is no denying another source of Reality. Only I'm not walking on a sunny path in Boston Commons, and the veil that has suddenly been lifted is not the one that separates me from the living being of the outside world. This time I'm walking down an unlit path into the dark world of my unconscious and the veil that is lifted is the one that has separated me from my own soul.

LIGHT.

…Eddie and Daniel came home and walked into the bedroom where I was writing. I felt alive again. I felt "normal," like I'm just here in my room at my computer on this beautiful afternoon like a normal person. I can't remember the last time I felt this way. Every muscle in my body was relaxed. I could feel incredible warmth flood through my heart, and I could *feel that my soul had never left me*. It was waiting for me. I *knew* that my soul loves me outside any sense of time or judgment.

I told the man I was working with, whom I will call T, about the writing. He said it was the most important thing I would ever do. I'm not sure I believed it was a repeatable experience, but I quickly discovered that all I had to do was write down a question and "They" were there to answer it from a perspective unlike any I had ever encountered.

I can feel that this life as I know it is only the outermost skin of what my existence is all about. I feel happy now sometimes. But I also notice that I am afraid to have this feeling, afraid something bad will happen, but mostly I feel I don't deserve to have this. Now They are saying,

It is not about having or not having, it only looks that way in this particular type of life you have entered. It is about letting go of all your pictures of what life is supposed to be and trusting Us. We do not have another way to say it for now. We are not people but We are translating into the personal for you. It is about giving up the little you and letting Us take you in Our arms. Being able to have something or not have it is just a vehicle of experience like everything else.

You are allowed to enjoy this life. You, in particular, need to enjoy this life right now. She needs a sunny place in the window to rest and recover, but you are no longer Her. You are afraid you have misheard Our words, but you have not. You fear you are presumptuous. Just listen. It is presumptuous to doubt! (We have a sense of humor, too.) You have crossed over a line. You can go back if you feel more comfortable with fear, pain, and uncertainty. We are teasing you. We love you. We are telling you again, you have no say over what is happening. Life says what happens. Your say is to move with life, not hold back, not doubt. You have never failed to listen in the past. It's just that it has taken you a very long time in your frame of time and it has involved so much pain. Your say is to move with the flow of the ocean, not against it. The ocean moves, with or without you. But We are not indifferent to your movement and that is why We are here. We have always been here.

Go toward love, toward acceptance but always of yourself at the same time. Go toward the heart. We cannot stress that enough. Go from your heart to the Heart and leave the rest to God and to Soul in its collective sense. You are all fragments of Soul and together you as Soul are God's presence in form. Stay very close to your heart right now. Love unconditionally and WITHOUT FEAR. Never again be afraid to LOVE, fully, with everything you have. It is not who you love or what you love that matters. It is THAT you love. That is what makes it unconditional. You didn't know it yet for yourself, and this lifetime has been about knowing it for you. So far. Don't worry about love, about a partner, about being loved as you tend to think of it. You ARE loved now.

We are glad you are noticing that you are coming back into your body. Strange, isn't it, to think that you are SUPPOSED to be in your body. But you are. If you have a body, you are supposed to be in it. It is as simple as that. There are reasons beyond what you can now imagine that you are supposed to be in a body, in just the very body you are in, no less. Meditate on that. Love that. Your body is a true miracle beyond your wildest imagination.

Forget about your belief that one measure of your healing is pain going away. Be in your body while you have it. Be in any moment while it lasts, any experience, any space, any feeling. Especially feel your body. Like We said, there are experiences you are supposed to have in this body that you have not been sufficiently in the body to have. There are visitations from God that are designed to come through bodies and they are unique experiences, not like any others. You humans often mistakenly understand these "spiritual" experiences to be unrelated to incarnation, but that is incorrect.

PAIN IS THE ABSENCE OF LOVE. REMEMBER THAT. Pain is the signal that Love is needed. It is as simple as that. Pain calls you to love. Embrace every experience. Every experience is sent to you for a reason. Every reason ends with Love. We are working on your body. Right now, We are working on your heart and your heart is moving energy into your throat and mouth. You have always known that something of an entirely different nature from the cries of pain you have had is trying to come out of your throat and mouth, and letting those cries come out has only been the very first step, like unclogging a pipe so that clear water can flow.

TRUST US. You trust Us by writing Our messages and by intentionally maintaining an awareness of what We have told you and by doing what We tell you to do. You have everything to gain and the more you do this, the more you will understand exactly what it is you have to gain. As yet, you have no idea.

We will always be here. You have no need to worry about that. We want you to write this and that is why We have come to you initially in this form. You don't realize how specifically designed these experiences are. There is nothing random about why We come to you this way. You will begin to see all life through another lens. You have steered yourself with impulses from the soul, from Us, with half-closed, doubting eyes. It is a hard road and a long road. Now you open your eyes and you don't exactly steer anymore. As We have said, the steering is an illusion anyway. Now you open your eyes and you move with the current that you find yourself in.

We are eternal. We have forever. You, in this form, do not, and that is exactly as it should be. Do not be afraid to let the old life go. It is like putting down your crutches and walking.

Amazing as all this is, as connected and alive as I can feel, I am often resistant to writing. I don't know why. I still feel lost, lost in a better place than before but I still feel totally alone. I still feel empty, just not as scared. I doubt everything about myself and in that space of doubt, I doubt this writing, too. I feel so weird, as if no one can know this about me, and now I have yet another secret that cuts me off from "normal." I have feelings like I will be accused and blamed, like I've done something terribly wrong.

Be again in your body. Don't leave through your mind or any other route. What you have never been able to grasp is the "presence" that can come through simply locating your consciousness in your body. That is what was lost in your early experience. Now, fortunately, you are at a point where you can both come back into the body and where you can see the pitfalls of leaving it, so that leaving is not so unconscious and not so attractive an option. A mind split off from the body and the emotions and the soul is a dangerous thing.

My parents called. They call every Sunday morning and we have the same conversation every time. "How's the weather? Oi, it's been so rainy here. How are the kids? How's your practice?" There's only one possible answer to every question. "Fine." And then we hang up.

Immediately I feel like not doing this anymore, like there's no hope for me, this is all a silly illusion anyway, and I'm nobody. Everything good just evaporates. I only feel safe in the smallest of worlds.

Look what love of self can bring to dark places. We heard your pain and your call for help. We are not indifferent OR ABSENT. When you look for what is good, what is growth producing and meaningful in any situation, you will see the very same situation entirely differently, and you will see where We are in the experience. There is NOTHING WRONG with what happened today!

I love what You say, but I can't see the good. I can't see the meaning.

*You are a being in a body on many levels; intended in this body to be an organism of spirit. **The whole package, just as it is, is spiritual, just as you were born into it.** It is a perfect, absolutely perfect creation for the transformation of certain energies, which We will not talk about now. The starfish that you put up in your office is a good enough representation of what We are talking about. There appear to be arms or differentiated aspects of functioning and in a sense there are, just as the starfish has legs. But they are connected in the middle and move out of their connection to the middle. You humans have, for the most part, lost your connection to the middle and so the little leg that looks like mind tries to operate all by itself or the little leg that looks like feelings seems to operate alone, and it only produces frustration and blockage. You knew you were not connected when you were very young and so out of that pain, you were drawn to "spiritual" practice as a way to bring the pieces of yourself together. Which was as good* *as it could have been. But We do not see that those particular spiritual practices as you like to call them really showed you that the different functions are meant to be one united, fused, perfectly blended **vehicle of conversion**. We do not see that those practices actually helped you bring those separate functions together in order to allow soul in you to awaken and manifest in the world.*

We are trying to tell you over and over again that your body and your mind and your feeling and your sex and your hand that paints and your eye that sees God in a flower petal are all little arms of the starfish held together by the central fact that you are alive in an incarnated form. We do not even want to say that you are incarnated into a body because essentially that is a misuse of words. You are incarnated into form, which is a very different concept. Let the center regenerate new legs. Forget everything you know about "mind" and about "emotion." And especially, forget everything you know about "spirituality." Grow new legs. This is not easy for you humans as you now are because you love your old legs and truthfully, We do understand. But We are telling you there is no particular "healing" for old legs that We are interested in talking about. You can get all that information from the current literature. You know a lot of it already and it is good. But you are asking for an answer to the question of what you are doing here in this life in this form, and We are taking this opportunity to tell you something entirely new.

*This is what you really must know. We are deliberately moving you out of the usual viewpoint, the psychological or "healing" viewpoint as you know it because "as you know it" is terribly, terribly limited. The point of your existence is **not** to become healed in the New Age sense, not to become that for which you have so longed all your life. Sorry, but the point of your existence is not to become a so-called "healthy, well-adjusted" person. **The point of your existence is, right now, to be pushed out of the cocoon of human development as you have learned it.** Remember, you have learned what you know from those who extracted knowledge from the accumulative side of human development and experience over time. What you have learned is by no* *means the whole truth. Now you are learning from another source entirely, from the un-incarnated side. You cannot know what that means now, but you know that something quite remarkable has happened, that We are opening up to you a perspective that has not been available before.*

I will never be able to express fully what it was like to hear these things so clearly stated within my own mind but not generated by any known part of myself. Awe is not a big enough word.

*You can be in awe. But never let fear keep you from coming through this door. We would wait, of course. As We said, We have forever. The point of your existence right now is to come over to the "other side," so that you may see there is no "other side," not in Reality. However, you must be in Reality to see this, to know this, to live and breathe this. We know you are asking how you achieve this. We know that you can feel what We say while We are saying it, but you want to know what you do in daily life to achieve it. **Open yourself into a moment to existence.** You see that We did not say **your** existence, but Existence. You, as the center of the starfish, **ARE the transmitter of existence**. You are to use all experience to remind you to move into the center. That is where We are.*

Much later on, very specific instructions would unfold, but the unfolding was in no way linear, and therefore it is impossible to present Their wisdom in any other way than exactly how it was given to me– gradually through my own life experience and the questions I asked.

Use all experience to remind you to move into the center. That is where We are. When you move into that awareness, you will feel love for humankind rising up inside you as if from nowhere. But it is not nowhere. It is real where it comes from. It is where We live all the *time. **Your whole organism is intended to be the vehicle of transmission of Divine Love.** And that love will move you out of the realm you have existed in all this time. That love will both enable the transmission, it will be the transmission, and it will be the instrument of regeneration We referred to before.*

We make Ourselves very small to reach down into the world of words. We are not the least bit disturbed by that. In Reality, there is no large or small, there is only distinction of PURPOSE. We make Ourselves into exactly what is needed. And you sense in yourself the contraction We use to reach you so that Our mind can open into yours. So much love is here for you.

A definite psychic experience produces the words. Something takes over inside me as if I am let into another realm that is more like continuous with me. I can actually feel the energy of this other realm work to find words in human language. Yesterday, it took my breath away and at the same time, I almost stopped because it was so overwhelming to have a "secret" that, if I let it, could take me back to feeling I will never fit in. But I hear You saying,

*Who cares? What will you gain by fitting in? When you lie on your deathbed, will you find happiness and fulfillment from fitting in or will you allow yourself the true fullness of knowing and being Home with Us consciously at that wonderful moment? Yes, wonderful moment. We are not saying you should not be close to others or find love among people. What We are saying is that you have an opportunity to go beyond the limits of what people tend to think this life experience is all about. You have the very same challenge you have always had, which is to **trust** yourself, to move freely within yourself, and not hold back, no matter what the doubts. You opened yourself to explore the pain. You could have been drinking, smoking, or watching TV. But you opened that door and went in, and now you are on a turn of the very same spiral of faith and trust and belief in yourself, only this time you are dealing with a very different kind of truth.*

*Can you feel it? To be both an "individual entity" and not individual in the same moment? The individual entity needs love. The not individual is **a part of love and needs nothing except to open and open.** The rest is done for you, through you, and with you as you allow it.*

I see that different truths apply at different times. There are no absolute truths in what I perceive, only partial truths. Perhaps that is the condition of incarnation, I don't know. So actually, one effect of being so deeply in touch with the un-incarnated realm is that I feel more accepting of different states in myself. I think acceptance is a key toward greater fluidity between my normal state of consciousness and this new realm of awareness. So sometimes I can be more accepting that this information has been unsettling to my status quo. Most of the feelings I have are that I am presumptuous and weird. But the more I write, the more I want to write. I want to share this with a few people, not because I think I am the bearer of some great message, but because I want to share more of myself and not always feel I am hiding a big part of my existence. I wish I felt that free. I so fear being perceived as presumptuous.

We are glad you are here and glad you are willing to take this risk. There is nothing to fear. There is no possible mistake. We are real, We are here, and We are not going away.

***

And so this is how my journey with Them began. There were no direct answers about the pain I felt; no suggestions for "cures," no psychological explanations or even words of encouragement, like, "Don't worry. Things will be better." I was taken out of my psychological world where I believe we still look for relief, for cures, as of course we should. But I'm not so sure any of us is comfortable *hanging out* with pain *too* long. I think the unstated goal is to get out of pain as quickly as possible and success is measured in those terms. I have measured my own "success" that way. Nor am I suggesting that pain is a value in and of itself. But what if we didn't fixate so much on alleviating it too quickly but rather encouraged a *willingness* to plumb its depths for gold and held *that* light for those in the darkest part of their tunnel? My apparent curse, which proved to be the greatest blessing, was that I didn't seem to have a choice.

What was conveyed to me had a quality of Love and Truth that was beyond anything "reassurance" could have given me. Through Them, I connected to a Source. No matter what I asked, They took me directly into the world of Soul, into a perspective that transformed the darkness of my pain and limited understanding into the *Divine meaning* of everything I was experiencing. From the very beginning, there was an understanding that everything, just as it is, is *for a purpose*.

And so I opened up the darkness I found in myself even further. I could not stop it. In a space of Truth, there is nowhere to go but into your own little truths, no matter how small, ugly, ignorant or even halfway intelligent and sincere they might seem to be. Whatever my Darkness was, They brought Light. And there was not one ounce of judgment ever conveyed, only the most Divine Wisdom that was in itself imbued with a Love completely unlike anything I had ever experienced. Their Love was both personal to me and beyond the world of personal altogether.

Chapter II

I asked Them about my relationship with M, someone I really wanted to be close to. But I had felt rejected and judged by her and as a result, sometimes I had unkind thoughts about her. I felt awful about this in light of the boundless Love that was being given to me.

You don't need to feel awful. You are not expected to be perfect. One aspect of incarnation is about learning. See what there is to learn from this experience. Look at the part that harbored unkind thoughts and see it as something that was under a shadow. When you lift a dark shadow and light comes in, there can be a moment of pain from the light. But the point is not to shut your eyes again. It is to acclimate yourself to the light. Do not be afraid to admit what you see. The truth cannot hurt you. Asking for forgiveness is a cumbersome way of saying, "I am willing to be with the truth of myself, I am willing to stand on and learn from every aspect of myself and I am not in control of how that learning comes about. I am only in control of offering myself up to that learning and receiving it." That is why, truly, another cannot "forgive" you for anything. All the other can do is be willing to be in his or her truth in relation to you. Stand in the truth in your own mind. This will teach you all you need to know.

You and she are not in each other's lives in just this way by accident. *Nothing is an accident. This understanding brings compassion where it has been hard to find. She has her own struggles, you have yours, and they mesh in just this way. Each obstacle, each stone in your path, is to be blessed. When you bless an obstacle from the heart, it ceases to be an obstacle. When you bless her seeming indifference or* *rejection, it will no longer be an obstacle to you, it will no longer cause you pain in the way it does now. This is the difference between the "small self" and the "large Self." The small self or **ego** deals with feelings, with the right and wrong of a relationship, with psychology. The "large Self" deals with the heart, with Soul, with MEANING and with Us. It deals with the meaning of what is occurring in any given relationship from the point of view of **what you came to learn** from the experience. The "right and wrong" of ego's world is very powerful and not to be argued with. It is to be ACCEPTED and LOVED and then, in the loving, you will find TRANSCENDENCE. There is no right or wrong here. There is only **what is** and what you can learn from it. Right now, you are learning that you are in each other's lives in just this way for a reason.*

I saw that part of that reason was for me to find a stronger foothold in my own truth and not to be shaken off center by another's response. I had been focused on the *right and wrong* of every relationship my whole life, on the good and bad of others and myself. Could all these experiences really be sent to me for the *purpose* of *learning* something other than that?

The words PURPOSE and MEANING kept coming into my mind last night as I was going to sleep. I saw that the *meaning* of something is the transformative bridge, not judgment of good, bad, right, or wrong, but the meaning and purpose I give it. I am continuing to work on the issue of holding to my own truth no matter what the response, and that might be the "meaning" of my relationship with M being difficult. I have believed I have to accept another's truth over my own if I want to have any chance of belonging, of being loved. And yet, in trying to stand on my own truth no matter what, I hear, "Sin of Pride!" screaming in my head.

*There will be many things along the way that will make you fearful and want to stop what you are opening up. That is part of the Way. We cannot say the challenge will be any the less as you go on. **The force of Soul guidance will become all-powerful, and the form will*** *struggle with whatever struggles remain for it to confront in this lifetime. Every one of these struggles is a blessing. The more you write, the more you will see that. This is the first step in understanding that form is a vehicle of conversion and transmission of energies* (the form is intended to convert the energies bound up in our ego experiences into soul consciousness and transmit the light and love of soul to the world around us). *You do not need to fear presumptuousness or egotism, for those qualities cannot pass beyond certain gates. The fact that you fear these things is fine for now but ultimately unnecessary and you will find it holds you back. We know you hear the call. You are moving toward a place where you STAND ON WHAT YOU KNOW, no matter how large or small in your frame of reference. That is not presumption. It is actually an aspect of Faith, of Spirit or Soul permeating form and expressing itself through form. That is not presumption. In Our eyes, and please look through Our eyes, it is a matter of becoming one with Us.*

*You and M have chosen each other on this road. There is a bond between you that goes way beyond present day events and dilemmas. Keep that as an overview. Nothing can hurt you. Your love in many ways has been tied to your pain. Do you see that? If you allow it to be released from your pain, it will merge with Our Love. If you release your love from the need for M's acceptance, you will see that just as there is a big Self and a small self, there is a big Love and a small love. When your love and compassion are tied to pain in another or in yourself, you are in a sense in the small love, the love that is a reflection of what **your** Hurt One needs. And in that sense, your love remains very self-centered and often blind to the reality of the other. It is not bad but it can be limited.*

*The MEANING of what is happening with M is that you are being pushed beyond that myopic point of view. Rather than sending love and compassion to another's pain or your own, rather than trying to fix anything, (which We say is not a bad thing in ordinary life), **there is an opportunity for you now to send love and compassion to another's PATH, to the road they chose to travel on this long Road Home, and*** *to your own Path as well. If you love your Path in its entirety, you will heal.*

Why do I still have so much anxiety? What should I do with it, and what is the purpose of it for me at this point?

The essential nature of all aspects of the ego is to be at war with itself. In your unconsciousness, you are caught in that trap over and over again. You feel something and don't want to feel it, know something and don't want to know it, see something and don't want to see it, whether it is of the personal or the societal or the global. When you feel anxiety and loneliness, you are in the small self, your ego nature.

Remember: the mind and the feelings of ego are cut off from the Source and run in circles around themselves. That was all they were ever meant to do. You MUST know that every time you use the small self as a springboard to Us, let Us say to you now– TO GOD—Yes, for We are only another vehicle on another level of what is God– **every time you use the small self as a springboard to GOD, you clear your channels, you receive from what is High, you make yourself more available to Be Of Service, you lessen the load of unconsciousness in the world, and you bring the light THAT IS WAITING TO SHINE, into one more dark corner of the Universe.** *You are given the opportunity to feel, every day if you like, the ecstasy of this. Take the doubts that linger, even now, in your mind, and hold them up to Our Love to be blessed and blown into the wind.*

I took that to mean that every time I allowed myself to step out of judgment and open to the meaning and purpose of experience, I was using my small self as a springboard to God. It was very hard to do. They were right. My small self was so bound to what I thought was good and bad, to what I wanted and didn't want.

And even so, even with the heart-pounding extraordinary Love that You pour into me, I wake up and there is the emptiness of repetitive, anxious thoughts running around in my head. I am as afraid today that You will leave me as I was when You first came.

*We are here. Do not be afraid. You have just begun the ascent of a very steep mountain with no equipment, maybe a walking stick for balance. You are being asked to have faith. That does not necessarily make it easy. Literally, you lay your life down. **You have chosen this road**. This is important and do not forget it. In this way, each day is a part of your ascent, each day is important in terms of your reconnection to PURPOSE. See it as a challenge, as a great opportunity. Hear God calling louder. Every effort you make is real. Every effort you make, whether you think it is effective or not, contributes to your growth and progress on the path.*

You humans are so achievement oriented in a production kind of way that you have lost sight of this. Everything counts in the great scheme of things. Part of faith is that you allow yourself to enter an unknown space without a "satisfaction guaranteed" sign on the door. In the darkest moment when the shadow falls like night, We are here with you and will always be. Our love is real. You do not walk this Path alone. You never have. Take Us with you in your heart. It is where We want to be, where We choose to be.

We have been here before! Begin to see where along the way your vision and Our vision have crossed paths. In the past, when you were afraid of "what you knew," you were having a hell of a time because We were informing you at many levels unseen. Therefore, you have made another step in allowing Us fully into your awareness.

*You think We are a miracle. **We are not a miracle. You are.** We are always here in this way. We are the sun. You are the flower that made its way up through a slab of cement. You think We are separate from you and therefore believe that We could leave you. We are as much a part of the organism as your heart or your mind or your big toe. In a* *sense, We are another organ, however not one that is visible to the eye. So when We are finally seen, it appears to be a visitation. Let Us say this again. Not everything you thought you knew was Reality. Incarnation is a design with a purpose far beyond what you have thought and We say again that certain visitations from God are intended to be transmitted through the vehicle that you understand to be your personage. BUT IN REALITY YOU ARE NOT BEING VISITED BY US, YOU ARE US AND WE ARE YOU. We will burn your doubts and your fears for you. Do not be afraid of this fire. It scorches the earth but it also renews it. It burns up the illusion that you are separate from Us.*

Last night was very intense for me. It was another one of those awe-inspiring times when you know that you are in the presence of something beyond anything you could ever have imagined. I have heard concepts before that relate to some of what You have told me, but this is so very different because I am *experiencing* what You say. The words are the translation of the experience. In the past, I would try to hold a certain thought in order to have an experience of it. This morning as I was lying in bed, I began to have that very gentle and subtle pulsing of golden light in my forehead and that changed into different kinds of pulses of very intense gold and orange circles of light that rose like little suns. But that isn't exactly it either. I just don't know other words. There was a quiet but definite heart reaction, and even in writing this again, I feel the energy intensely in my throat and mouth coming up from my heart.

My days are better. I feel good a lot of the time. Since my emotional pain has subsided, I am less attached to other people's pain. I have more faith, more belief that they can get through their pain now and so it doesn't seem so enormous. And my bad feelings about myself are subsiding, too.

You "reach down" to others, so to speak, as We reach down to you. **You are a part of others as We are a part of you.** *We are not talking about "individual beings or entities." We are not individual entities.*

We are a state of consciousness. You are a state of consciousness. This is very difficult to understand because you have learned to think concretely in this type of lifetime. We are saying that concrete thinking is only one very small aspect of what the human brain is capable of. Try to see this so that you can begin to work with your brain to perform other functions. When We say We are messengers, We are like waves washing over a particular aspect of consciousness, changing it as We go. You are all messengers working every moment to refine your message.

Chapter III

For two weeks out of every month, I had severe pain at the base of my spine that no one could diagnose. I survived on high doses of Ibuprofen. Like everything else, I asked about the pain in my body. This question opened up the beginning of a whole new understanding of the extent to which my mind, body, emotions, and spirit were all connected. It was not meaningless nor was it accidental that I was having very powerful sensations in certain parts of my body. (Much more would be revealed to me about the connections—for us all- as time went on.) About the pain at the base of my spine, They said–

*The body, as We have said, does not exist as a separate entity apart from the mind, emotions and spirit. The pain serves to alert you to the fact that the Receptive Feminine in you needs assistance. The part of you that can **receive** has blockage and therefore as a result you are having difficulty **transmitting** what you are intended to transmit. The Masculine Active, which is the transmitter, therefore also needs help. Flood the whole area with golden yellow light.*

*The energy that is blocked is your "**generative**" energy. **Trust that the pain in your body has been given to you, as all else has been given to you, for your greatest illumination along your Path. Use pain to call light into your organism.** It is a gift that an area blocked to reception is now being opened. The way the Universe works is that when blockage (which is a condensation of ego energies) is removed or* *broken up, Light pours in of its own accord, just as atmosphere pours into a vacuum if the opening is made. And you can now **agree to participate** in allowing the Light in. You can call it into your body.*

You have noticed that there has been a great deal of energy in your heart, throat, and mouth, especially when you are contacting Us. These parts of your body are areas that have been blocked as well as the base of your spine, which is where you are now experiencing physical pain. As soul seeks to shine its light through you, it focuses first on the areas most blocked and that is why so much energy is pouring into these specific places. While it sometimes feels like pain, it is actually the discomfort of old energy blocks being broken up.

The next day I was leaving my house for an appointment in the middle of my workday when suddenly the vibration in my heart, throat, and mouth became so intense I had to stand by the front door and just take it in. My heart was vibrating as I heard these words spoken in my head– *IMPULSE TAKES FORM*. It was as if a blast of energy from a cosmic realm hit my consciousness like a bolt of lightning. *IMPULSE TAKES FORM*. Then I heard You say–

*This is a way of seeing and interpreting behavior—you can look at the **forms** of behavior and easily trace them back to the **impulses** that create them.*

At first, this statement seemed to apply to ordinary behavior. Specifically I understood that all my resistance, like trying to find anything else to do besides sit down and write, was the result of an impulse to block—to block awareness, to block out the discomfort of leaving my known world, to block out the forces of self-doubt and fears of presumption. I heard You tell me that me all behavior could be read by looking at the *impulses* behind any particular manifestation. But my heart was pounding out of my body and I felt I was in another world. Energy shot through me. The magnitude of what I saw went way beyond human functioning. I caught an outline of the construction of our **universe.** The energy and the understanding behind those words was this: **ALL FORM** IS THE MANIFESTATION OF AN **IMPULSE,** OF AN **INTENT,** FROM FAR OUTSIDE THE LIMITS OF OUR KNOWN WORLD.

ALL of Creation issues forth from a COSMIC INTENTION. There is Meaning and Purpose way beyond the events and challenges of my personal life.

REVELATION.

***

Let me say something about this word Revelation. It is one thing when light shines into a dark place you know well, like that place of total emptiness when all you want to do is land in a well-lit living room on a couch in someone's arms. It is one thing when the Light that shines tells you something *did actually happen* that made you feel that utter desolation all your life. But it is a *whole other experience* when Light illuminates a part of the structure on which your entire known world is built, when you suddenly catch a glimpse of a law of the Universe and you see that there is a known and knowable *intention* informing every manifestation we are capable of perceiving. That was what that moment was for me. And once again, I had no idea that this was just the very beginning of an outline of a structure for human beings that They would share with me—**through my experience of myself.**

Many of the essentials of this outline do not appear in this book because they unfolded over time. The groundwork is laid in my initial experiences and writing, but the specifics do not emerge until later. You will be able to find this information in future books.

Let me say something more about this word Revelation. It sounds so biblical and in fact, as I received this word it *felt* biblical, but not like anything I was familiar with from the little bit of exposure I had to the Old Testament, and not like anything I associated with Christianity which seemed to be all about dogma and sin and repentance. It seemed that for reasons yet unknown, I was being given a cosmically expansive, unconditionally loving, and first-hand interpretation of spirit in *biblical* terms!

Chapter IV

Oddly enough, or perhaps not oddly at all, with every blast of Light that came to me, another aspect of what had lay hidden in my personal experience of darkness became more intense and more compelling. I was bouncing wildly between cosmic panoramas and the small black basements of my existence. AND, I was hearing words and sensing meanings so biblical in nature that I felt myself slipping backward into a forbidden and dangerous relationship to the Church. All of this completely outside anything my Jewish intellectual mind could explain.

I'm having awful feelings of the conservative elements in society burning me at the stake, not literally in this life, but more like I am at risk with this information. I am aware that the resistance I feel is not all from doubt.

These were not idle thoughts. They were sensations powerfully felt in my body and taking shape in my mind. I was beginning to have a different kind of memory…

You saw into a corner of Our consciousness and moved back. What you saw is that this information is not to be used solely in your personal life and that frightened you. You do not have to worry about this now. You are asked only to work with what is emerging now. That is all anyone is ever asked.

*Listen to your own inner voice in everything. Listen to all the impressions that are flooding in on you. Make this conscious in your daily life. Your soul wishes, if you allow it, to move with far-reaching strokes. The reason why there is so much energy in your heart and throat is that **you wish to speak**. Your ability to speak is NOT DEPENDENT ON THERE BEING A RECEPTIVE AUDIENCE. Never confuse the two. You speak ultimately for the sake of your Soul, not for the sake of any particular listeners.*

And so both my inner world AND my outer world were blasted open. Everything I knew myself to be- little Phyllis Leavitt from Plainfield, New Jersey, who thought she would have been lucky to fit into a nice suburban home with the Jewish doctor husband, little Phyllis Leavitt who at that time in 1995 could barely leave her house where she lived alone with her children- that Phyllis Leavitt was shown a law of the Universe and was told she was someday going to be talking about it to the world!

I am so frightened by hearing that I am not to use this information solely for my personal life. **I'm not there yet**, wherever it is You are pointing. If Impulse Takes Form, is this what You are talking about?

Right at that time, I went to a workshop on Dissociative Disorders and the issue of therapists being sued for encouraging false memories in clients came up.

In the middle of the workshop, I had a wave of anxiety flood over me about being *persecuted* for my beliefs. I could feel the terrible dilemma of being at the mercy of forces beyond my control and being persecuted for beliefs I could not abandon. I really don't know if this is just a normal feeling response to what is going on today of a reactionary nature or if there is something here that may have to do with some past life experience. You told me I am getting messages every day from the Soul part of me and I feel now that something very deep and old is being stirred up. I once went to a psychic to ask about my lifelong desire to write. She told me that in some other lifetime, it had been very dangerous for me to write, but she wouldn't say more.

Here I stand at the same old crossroads, afraid of what I know.

*Is it clear to you that you have the opportunity, in this lifetime, to finish the work of many lifetimes? You **are** on Trial, but not in the earthly sense, not to be proven bad or wrong and not to be punished. You are on trial in one of the biggest trials of your present life. This has been a theme in many lives. You can deny Us if you wish. As you can see, there does not need to be a fire burning at your feet for you to feel the burning of the dross around your Soul. You have been in that position before and now you came back to try again. You asked and We answered. We told you We will not go away and We **will not** go away. Your trial is one of Faith. Your trial is one of Action based on Faith. When you are presented with Knowledge, you must use it.*

Now, coming back to your sense that perhaps in another lifetime you were persecuted for your beliefs, that there was life-threatening danger associated with expressing your truth, We ask you to tune in to these impressions and let yourself know what you know.

I actually believe it is true. I am so grateful for Your presence. Please forgive me for the times I cannot reach out to You.

There is nothing to forgive. We see your organism much more clearly than you do. You are working on many more levels than you realize, and We have absolutely no criticism of the process– quite the opposite. Out of love for you, We want to say that it will serve you to see every feeling, every thought, every frustration, as well as every high point, as part of your work. What you call lapses do not appear that way from Our side. Please let the love available to you in this statement come into your being.

I had never been interested in past lives. A psychic once told me about a past life but it had no meaning for me. I figured anyone could make up a story and I would never know if it was true or not. It seemed to me I would need to see the past life for myself to believe it and I never had the interest to pursue it. But now something undeniable and unstoppable was pressing on my psyche and it didn't seem to come from the life I knew as Phyllis.

On a break today, I sat in my office thinking about my sense of past lives and what it would be like to trust what comes up in me. And I heard You say,

*You can only get answers on the inside. So if Doubt is the Lion At The Door, you may have to pass through those gates again and again. There is no knowledge for you on the outside. There is no one who can tell you other than to direct you back to yourself. This is your Trial–to take what is offered from within without knowing in the mind of the small self, which is **incapable of KNOWING** in the sense We mean. The only proof of that knowledge for you is in your experience of that knowledge. **The task is to TAME the mind of the small self so that eventually it relinquishes its hold on doubt and denial, comes to recognize a power greater than itself, drops its defenses, and lays its weapons down of its own accord.***

The Path is laid out. You can travel it now or later. You have an internal Teacher that is magnetizing to you all the experiences you need. It is when you don't listen that you are LOST.

I start to feel like I'm crazy, that my life is being over-run by You, but even when I say this I know that nothing could be better than having You be the center of my life. I'm sorry for my stupid thoughts and fears. It is difficult to realize that with all the Love I have received from You, I still do not walk around radiating love or even feeling love a lot of the time.

Your feelings, whatever they are, are YOUR personal teacher. You humans do not all have the same feelings because you do not all have the same Paths. You need your particular feelings as a road map through experience until you don't need them anymore.

Love comes not as you have thought. Open yourself to experiencing a new definition of Love. **Love comes, at the present time, through accepting and embracing the Pattern you are working out.** *Love comes through seeing your being in its exquisite intricacy of PURPOSE. Love comes when you understand yourself as* **a vehicle of soul** *and therefore you understand that all creatures and all non-human manifestations in form are also vehicles of soul. You cannot have the kind of Love We are talking about, which is intelligent or Wise Love, until you grasp that.*

So you want to ask about this pattern of loneliness. You **chose** *this pattern. Please be aware of this. You came to connect to the other side and you chose not to be immersed in many entangled relationships for the purpose of hearing this call from your own Soul. However, it is not intended for this to be isolation. Rather–DISCERNMENT. It is a SOUL pattern specific to you at this time. It was not intended to be a life pattern in terms of a punishment or limitation. It was a Soul choice intended to help you on your Path. It was intended to be experienced as a tool. Discernment is a key word for you. Being alone has been a Path Clearer. As the Path clears and you find yourself in an open field, there can be others. You are not bound to loneliness. At the present time, you are bound to Discernment.*

***

I'm in a very scary place. I'm trying to do it differently. I was feeling very panicky and I just allowed the feelings to be there. I didn't try to change them. I just faced them and accepted them the best I could. It was very powerful what happened for me. The fear did die down and I felt more confident that I could face fear in the future. But fear and doubt still take over so easily. What is coming up in this writing is extremely challenging to me and I feel I am on the very edge of myself with it.

They were talking to me about laws of the Universe and persecution and sharing with others a "truth" that seemed to challenge a "Church" I had no relationship with and barely any knowledge of in my present day life. When They pointed to past lives, I had physical sensations that were outside the realm of reason and completely beyond my control. And all the while, They poured a love into me I had never known and all of this, yes, took me to the very edge of myself.

You can see doubt and fear as the same. Fear blocks the door to receiving, to the Receptive, the Feminine. Doubt masks Fear. When you doubt, you feel safe from the fear lurking beneath it. What are you afraid of?

I am afraid of being nothing, of thinking I might be okay and finding out I'm not.

I am afraid of being a failure.

I'm afraid I'm a sorry excuse of an unloved woman.

I'm afraid of being presumptuous in even thinking I have this experience of You and receiving wisdom from You that is completely beyond the capacity of my ordinary mind to think up. Okay, I say, I'll have Faith but just let me hold onto a little Doubt just in case.

I'm afraid of being accused of the "Sin of Pride."

All of this is what you came here to work with, what you chose and were chosen to work with. *It is not an easy path. Faith will take you* *very far. Allow all these fires to burn. Do not fight them, do not run from them, and do not fear them. You see, ultimately you cannot work out Soul Pattern and Soul Path through the consciousness of the small self. This is a very difficult concept to grasp. The fear and doubt you are working with are not resolvable on the level of the small self, the personality.*

I was beginning to understand that what soul is working out through the tendencies, beliefs, and experiences of our ordinary lives is often quite different from what we strive for as personalities. As a personality, I wanted to be loved and often "gave myself away" in hopes of achieving that. As a soul, I was trying to stand on my truth *with or without acceptance*. I saw that within the very difficulties we face as personalities, the outline of our Soul Pattern and Path could become visible, like a luminous substructure around which our lives take shape and to which we can return as a guide and map back to soul itself. This was an emerging luminous substructure unlike anything I had ever seen or heard of in any previous "spiritual" work I had done. I saw the beginning of *my* soul pattern emerging through sensations of persecution, fears of speaking a "truth" I could not deny, whether personal or about soul and God, that was at odds with the powers that be. And as for the idea that I chose and was chosen to walk this path—well, more about that later.

*One of the challenges facing the human race today is both accelerated and at the same time blurred by the advances in technology and the sheer power man has created at this level of existence. **The challenge is to make the distinction between human creative potential on the level of the small self– which is manifested primarily as intellect, will power, complex emotion and construction of new material forms–***

and human creative potential on the Soul level. *The fear of this very departure—from models of success and belonging through development of the small self—fear of this very departure is a specific part of what you came to work through in this life.*

We love you.

Chapter V

Let me say here that there were so many strands of experience that came together at the same time that it may appear that no sooner have I opened up one subject than another apparently unrelated one follows. But I believe you will see that they all weave together with a logic and a perfection that at the time my conscious mind had no way to grasp.

All along I was continuing to work in therapy with a man I have called T–as in Teacher– because he was a powerful teacher for me in more ways than I could ever have imagined in the beginning of our relationship. I was continuing to work on memories of abuse in this lifetime with T, though our work together had expanded to include the perspective of my writing, all of which I was sharing with him. It wasn't exactly therapy. I understood it to be a combination of deep inner child work and a type of shamanic work T was trained in. Whatever it was, it was powerful. For the very first time, I felt totally safe with another human being to go down into the darkest, scariest places in myself. And it was an incredible gift that he so naturally went with me to the places of greatest light as well.

T has become very interested in what You have to say. He wants to share it with other people. At first, I was very hesitant. Then finally I said he could share it but ONLY if my name was not on it. I feel abject terror at the thought of anyone knowing **I** am writing this. I keep hearing the word "heretic" in my head. I feel like at any minute, men will be coming for me. I can see their angry, accusing, but indifferent faces. I feel totally unsafe even in my own house. Sometimes in my office I look out the sliding glass door, sure I will see them coming up the path. I feel I am not totally in present time when these feelings come, but there is adrenalin surging through my body. I'm feeling crazy.

And now I'm thinking about the letter I wrote to my parents telling them I want to take a break from talking to them. It's just too crazy making to talk about the weather every Sunday morning and then go to therapy the next day and shake and cry. I can't pretend I'm okay. I can't pretend anything these days. I told them I was working on sexual abuse and while I didn't come right out and say I thought they were a part of it, I didn't say they weren't either, and obviously if I don't want to talk to them right now, I'm implying *something* and I guess they must hear it. It took a lot for me to write the letter but I can't say I feel any better for having done it. I haven't heard from them, but I know they are upset with me.

I feel I will never be done being the problem one, the misfit. Everything I am doing is totally outside their known world. Therapy in any form is outside their world of books and perfect order and concerts and routine, The New York Times and a drink in the den at the end of every day. My world is only the slightest pretense of order, and I don't read anymore. And all I have experienced with You is *totally* outside any world I think they would even want to know. I wouldn't know where to begin if I were to tell them, or pretty much anyone for that matter.

*Remember, Phyllis–your parents, your practice, your children, your art, your writing, all your relationships—ALL are **vehicles of*** *experience*. *And Phyllis is the particular vehicle through which you have these experiences. We use the word vehicle wisely because a vehicle moves from one place to another and takes its driver, who is both driver and passenger, from one place to another. This movement can be mostly Horizontal in a given lifetime or it can be Vertical. Eventually the movement will become Vertical for all life forms. At this particular place on your Path, and this place exists on all Paths, you are given the opportunity to cooperate with the Vertical impulse. See yourself both driving the vehicle and being driven. See yourself as the vehicle. See that a different density of energy is required to make the movement Vertical. These are the best words We can find for you at the moment.*

Burning is the process of lessening the density so that movement becomes Vertical and energy rises. **When you listen to a given impulse from within and when you follow that impulse, you move energy that is tightly held on the Horizontal Plane (in the personality) and this gives you the opportunity to extract the energy contained in that experience for use by your soul**. *Every time you agreed to go deeper into buried memories and struggled to believe them, you were burning this energy. Every time you write, you are burning this energy. You are burning through or burning up all resistance the personality presents to your listening to that call of soul from within. And it is in burning up that resistance that you extract the energy held in your Horizontal Plane* (personality) *experience. This is what you are doing here with your parents. You are listening to the call of soul to hold to your truth in the face of your fears of hurting them or becoming more of an outcast. The power of that call is causing the resistance—fear and self-doubt—to be "burned," like fuel, and the energy released moves "vertically." This means it is now available to soul to create soul consciousness* **within** *the vehicle— which is you.*

You extract this energy by speaking your truth regardless. You break up the blockage in your mouth and throat and make all that energy *available to soul by **speaking**. Now or later. Soul waits for you and there is no blame.*

The message behind that was that we each break up the energy held in our ego experience in our own individual way, and that the place to begin is wherever we find ourselves called to something in our present day life but encounter resistance (internal or external)– obstacles, fears, or other blocks. More specific instruction on how to identify and break up this solidified ego energy will unfold as the writing continues.

Well, in that vein, I had an interesting experience today. I ended up making the split second decision to tell my friend J a little bit about this writing. When I spoke, I felt very enlivened and connected to myself. It was a feeling that I recognized from many previous experiences where I spoke my truth, like when I read the poetry I had written about my divorce, or when I shared my experiences in the desert, or when I talked about my memories to certain people. I was really struck by how different I felt after that conversation with J. Typically, I want to focus the conversation on the other person because I am ashamed of being seen as this empty, unlovable person. Anyway, I broke through that. *I was who I am*, and the difference was remarkable. And I remember saying to myself, Phyllis you have to hold onto this, don't forget it.

*Your truth and your aliveness **are the same**. Do you see that the impulse to tell your story– **to speak**– is the impulse to find US, to be with US, to live from US? Isn't it really quite beautiful that since childhood you were aware of the impulse to write your internal truth, that looking back you see that impulse has never left you, your **Soul** has never left you, and We have never left you?*

You asked about your parents and We have shared with you that they are a vehicle of experience. Your parents are a Symbol, In The Flesh, of the Experience of Persecution that you are working out. Hear these words very carefully, remembering that their meaning is far greater than you now know. Your parents are an externalized aspect of the Lion At The Gate. You must pass through them as a part of your Trial. That is why you keep coming back to the issue of telling them your truth. You cannot write your story without telling them your truth. You have known this for quite some time. This is a perfect part of your Path. There is more to tell about the Experience of Persecution, but that is for another time.

There is more doubt coming up in me than usual, more fear than ever of making anything about this writing visible. Maybe it's in reaction to what You are saying about persecution. **What kind of Path am I on?** The feeling of being safe only when I am hidden is huge. There is a tremendous feeling that my life will never be the same, which in my head and even in my heart, I can believe will only be a positive thing, because You are only a positive thing, but the fear is tremendous and I can see that it is translated directly into doubt and a desire to disconnect from what You are saying.

The more I wrote, the more I allowed myself to explore even the most unwanted thoughts and feelings, the more I began to see the outline of the *pattern* my soul had taken on, the skeleton around which my various lifetimes had been fleshed out. I saw that this pattern and path are "knowable" for anyone who seeks this understanding, and the first place to look is at our strengths, our callings, and the obstacles we encounter within and without.

Remember the feeling you experienced in telling J about your writing? That is what awaits you on a scale you have not yet imagined. Remember that. Do not push yourself. This is important. Let what has been communicated to you today sink into your conscious awareness. Let it, with great Love from Us, permeate your being slowly, in a timing that is right for you. You know exactly where you are on your Path, more than you have ever known before. There is no running on this Path. There is no time on this Path. There is only connection and Love on this Path. As you connect, you will move.

What You say is so huge. It takes me into the grand scale of this little life I think I am living and yet, at the same time, I feel this very young, infantile part of myself come up over and over again, an embarrassingly baby part of me that feels helpless and just wants to be taken care of. If I were in my therapy mode, I would say I am regressing. Ugh! It leaves me feeling as if everything else in my life is a sham—my work, and especially You. How can I be this infant and at the same time be here with Your Divine presence?

*Our focus is on helping you see the things that are making it difficult for you to operate from a connection to Us. What you are calling an "issue" with an infant part of yourself is only a mask for the real issue. The **real** issue is about the **WOMAN** in you who has not been allowed to emerge. The Impulse to allow the Woman to emerge is pushing on your psyche. As you RECEIVE from Us, the old vehicles for expression no longer fit the format needed to TRANSMIT what you are now receiving. **The other side to Reception is Transmission**. What is being Received cannot be Transmitted by the small self. That is why the adult Feminine is pushing on your psyche. And you will keep magnetizing the experiences that will show you all that is in the way. The experience you had with J shows you what it can feel like to speak from the Woman in you.*

*We want to help you understand what We mean by "Woman" because your thinking is too conditioned by modern standards of style. We are not talking about dress, weight, or even a "feeling" of being a woman. We are talking about WOMAN, the FEMININE. The FEMININE LEADS WITH THE RECEPTIVE AND MOVES TO THE ACTIVE OR EXPRESSIVE. The MASCULINE LEADS WITH THE ACTIVE OR EXPRESSIVE AND MOVES TO THE RECEPTIVE. **You are faced with the challenge of moving into the Feminine, the ultimate***

Receptive, in order to awaken the Masculine and Transmit what is yours to transmit. *And therefore, all that has been in your way of embracing the Feminine will be presented to you.*

I am feeling there is irritation in Your voice as You speak. I have never heard this before.

*You are hearing it this way because you believe We can only appear in one form. But it is not irritation. It is **power**. There are all kinds of expressions of Love in your world. And this is **Love with a Sword**. **Love With a Sword cuts through.** If you wish to travel this road, you must be able to SEE Love in all its FORMS, accept Love in all its FORMS, and you must be able to EXPRESS Love in all its forms.*

Love is NOT one of a number of emotions. LOVE IS THE CREATOR, and the CREATOR has created and continues to create ALL MANNER OF FORMS. LOVE IS MANIFESTED IN ALL FORMS. LOVE IS NOT AN EMOTION. IT IS THE POWER AND THE FORCE AND THE WISDOM AND THE PURPOSE OF THE CREATOR BEING EXPRESSED IN EVERY CORNER OF THE UNIVERSE. WHEN WE SAY GOD OR THE CREATOR LOVES, WE ARE SAYING GOD IS WIELDING THE TOTAL AND COMPLETE EXPRESSION OF THE DIVINE ON EVERY LEVEL OF BEING.

*Therefore, you are to no longer see Love as the other side of Hate. **There is no other side of LOVE**. Love, which brought this world into being and which will, in time, take it out of being, is beyond the reach of Hate. Hate is one half of a Duality in ego consciousness, a condition of the Horizontal Plane, a force to be contended with. LOVE IS GOD. THIS IS THE BIG PICTURE. YOU MUST KEEP THIS WITH YOU AS YOU WORK on the small picture. More exactly, this is another lens through which to see the microcosm you dwell in. WE ARE NOT SAYING HATRED HAS NO POWER ON THE MANIFEST PLANE, BUT THAT IS THE ONLY PLANE ON WHICH IT HAS POWER.*

LOVE IS THE CENTER OF THE CREATOR'S STAR. The Sword is one leg, Compassion is another, Wisdom is another, Service is another, Building is another, and Communication is another.

Last night was another one of those times that I felt if there was a doubt creeping in that I am making this up, it is again pushed back. I *experience* what You say as You say it. It vibrates inside my heart, inside my whole self.

I felt You. I had a glimpse of **OMNISCIENCE**.

Chapter VI

These are some of the initial threads that were slowly coming together—There was my child self that kept tapping into an unclear but terrifying Path of Persecution that was somehow related to my parents and triggered by them. There was the Woman in me who was slowly getting the sense that her life experience was meant to be the vehicle for something more than her expectations of a happy marriage, and that she was working her way toward sharing with others some vast emerging "truth" she was receiving. There was the relationship with T that at that time was instrumental in helping me bridge that gap between the two. And there was You, who told me in countless ways to bow to everything that was happening, to stay with my truth and follow it, to have faith in my own soul.

I can see all this clearly now. At the time, I was just "in it," swinging back and forth between extreme states of profound connection, utter disconnection, ecstasy, and terror. Slowly the threads began to weave together—the fear of heresy, the deep need—the *impulse*- to speak pushing up against the terror that my truth would kill me, the constriction in my mouth and throat, the defenses of hiding, self blame and doubt, and fears of persecution stirred up by the conservative elements of society.

The *impulse* to speak and the *impulse* to silence myself any way I could came face to face in my psyche. Those apparently conflicting impulses could be "read" but I couldn't quite see the fabric emerging back then because I was so swept up in a whirlwind of fear. I couldn't quite distinguish the force of my soul pushing through lifetimes of experience in ego consciousness. *They* helped me sort it all out– one day, one issue, one theme at a time. And as always, the themes They brought to light extended way beyond my personal experience to the *human experience*. It was almost as if my personal life was a template for something way beyond my particular personal story. It looked like the patterns running our lives are knowable, not just from the perspective of our early conditioning, but also from the perspective of our soul's evolutionary path.

So I thank You for continuing to trust me with Your presence. I want to say that I do not feel worthy but I know I can't say that. I will try my best to show my gratitude by not running away, even when I want to. I see that everything I have sought to both embrace and run away from is a part of my Path. I'm taking more chances telling people about this writing and my experience of You.

I get the message from You that **the whole Path is contained inside myself** (inside each of us), **that everything in me is the Path and therefore there is nothing to run from, nowhere to go, and nothing not to embrace. I hear You say that all the worlds meet when you embrace all that you are.** I see the most exquisitely beautiful picture of a Buddha in my head. He is dark, his face is peaceful and perfect, and his hands are palm to palm above his head. I see him as a Temple. And the message is that I am to become a Temple to myself. You are saying this like a command:

You Be A Temple unto Yourself. See yourself as sacred in everything, everywhere. If you do nothing else in your life, do this.

I understood that there are times when one moves out into the world and times when one goes within, but one never leaves the Temple of oneself in all that. I understood that everything I need is within me, the whole path is within me, *is* me. There is nowhere to go. I looked at my body in the bathtub and I heard You say that it really does not matter at all if a person is fat or thin, that the body is an essential part of that Temple and to hold it sacred, treat it as sacred.

What We are saying is that when you have the opportunity to fly, try not to walk the old rough road. And because wings are not an accepted means of travel in your present-day world, you feel that you must keep them hidden, you are afraid to know you have them, you do not even know you have them. We are here to tell you– you have them. Once you fly, you will never land the same way again. But you are not quite at that point. You are like a little plane trying bravely to take off, still going up and down over the runway, wheels touching and bumping, then up again, down, and up... Please hear this: What you are looking for is not on the ground, as you know it. We want you to feel this in your heart and in your throat and in every corner of the universe of your being. Go into the Temple of yourself. If you do nothing else in life, and you see, don't you– THERE IS NOTHING ELSE IN LIFE– do this. DO THIS. This life is truly not what you think. It never was.

I got a letter from my mother. She said I am breaking my father's heart. Not hers. His. I'm trying to hear You. I'm trying to listen, but there is so much terror inside this Temple that is me. The panic attack today– it seems like there is a very deep belief that I really did something wrong and that something very bad will happen to me. I am paralyzed with fear and anxiety.

*While the frightened one inside you was the doorway to understanding what happened to you in your present life, **she is equally the gateway*** *to understanding Life Beyond Form. She is the doorway to soul, and soul will show you where you have become stuck in your Horizontal Plane experience so that you can enter the World Beyond Form. You must go through her in every aspect. She is a Gate you must pass through. Embrace her.*

*We try to give you the feeling of flying, of the world you are leaving and the world you are entering. We work on the inner side so that you may know the experience of other worlds within your own universe. The panic and anxiety are signals that **there is more to know about the world you are leaving.***

*We are here with you. This feeling of Dread Terror that comes over you comes from both this life and from previous lives. It appears to you overwhelmingly bigger than Reality in the present moment because it is not only from the present life. The past is coming back to be "integrated." It has a message and a meaning. The message is, **Something big enough to produce this Dread Terror happened.** It is not that We or your Soul wishes you to be terrorized. We wish you to come back into yourself and **be with what is there, to pass through this Gate.***

It feels like there is no choice then but to believe that the abuse I remember from this life is real. I know the enormity of the distress I live with. My present life does not reflect the aliveness, love, adventurousness, and creativity I know are in me. It seems my real aliveness can come out in only very circumscribed situations, and even so, the fearful, constricted part often obliterates it.

But I need help because right now I want to get up and walk away from this whole process. Where are You taking me? I just need to hear Your voice.

We see a Cross as the symbol for where you are. Not a crucifixion as people tend to think about it in the flesh, but a Cross in the sense of a very deep and pronounced coming together of two very opposite forces that converge in a central point, which is also in the symbol of the Cross of Jesus Christ. The Cross is a symbol for the convergence, in form, of you and Us. It is also the symbol of the Path of Persecution, but that has a meaning other than the one you associate with it.

*What if you just have Faith in yourself, Faith in your process, Faith in your senses, Faith in your body, Faith in your intuition, Faith in your Spirit to guide you where you need to be? What do you imagine would happen to you if everything you have learned through all these avenues of yourself were true? **Both the felt sense of the abuse and the felt sense of Us?** Think about it. Don't run away.*

Do you know that when Christ was carrying the cross, he was not suffering? He was with Us. He had already chosen his Path. It was not forced upon him. He moved consciously and with great Faith along that road to the very end of that road, which has no End. And We were with him to the very end of that road that has no End. You still labor under the illusion that you could have another road than the one you are on. You still believe that your "cross" is a burden and you wish you could put it down. No. It is not in truth a burden or an infliction. Your cross is no different from Christ's cross. The only difference is that you have not picked it up in consciousness and in faith and in total surrender to the unseen Love of God that inhabits all ways. You do not believe God will love you that much. You do not believe anyone will be there in the end.

The Cross is as you experience it. You can believe it is a burden and a suffering forced on you from without or you can understand that it is your greatest gift that you carry as far as you are told to carry it until you can lay it at the feet of the One from whom you came forth. Your doubt and fear about your memories will be there as long as you need them to be. And they will disappear when you are ready to pick them up and walk with them, when you no longer need to ask how far you need to go, when you no longer care, when you can pick them up and carry what you have been given just because God and Soul have asked you to.

119

How does a person actually discover that his cross is no different from Christ's cross? That you and Christ are one? How do you actually **experience** *this and not just hold it as a beautiful concept in your mind or even in your heart? You discover this by actually picking up your cross and carrying it as Jesus did. We will show you exactly how to do this, but you start with understanding that* **whatever has been most difficult is an aspect of the cross you came to carry.** *We are here to help you uncover exactly what your cross is. As yet, you only have glimpses. We will give you all the instructions you need.*

I was so deeply affected by what You said. I feel like I am worshipping in a **real** church. I feel as if I am kneeling at the foot of a Biblical altar and a great Presence comes down from above and blesses me. And while I am with You it is the only place I want to be. My heart longs for You to take me Home, now. It is so hard to be here, in this life and in this person I am. The ordinary Phyllis just wants to be a normal person. She just wants to have a garden and a husband and to laugh a lot and be at ease inside her skin. More than anything, I want to wake up and feel good in the morning and I almost never do. This can't be the way I am supposed to live.

Does it occur to you that perhaps you are now able to embrace the anxiety in a way not possible before? Can you see the panic and anxiety as the last hurdle in your healing? This has been your particular path on the **Path of bringing Spirit and Form into Union. This is symbolized by the Cross.** *The "pain" of knowing what you know, and all the places you have stopped on the way, have been your journey with a Cross on your back. They have been your Stations of the Cross. Even this part of the journey can be done with Grace. You see this now. When you reach the mountain, when you* **stand** *on the Cross, that particular part of the journey is over, and a completely different journey begins. It has to do with Embracing the Way. This is the Way of Jesus.*

Forget about a "normal" life. Do these words sound familiar? Give it all to God. You have been asked.

And still I see my Path as one of unending suffering. I know it seems a contradiction, but as much light and love from You as has been given to me, and there has been *so* much, and much more than I ever had before, I still see my Path as taking me deeper and deeper into pain and I am so afraid.

*It is not suffering. It is transformation. The Cross is a symbol of The Way. Your experience in this world, on the Path, is in a continual process of transformation or conversion, not conversion to a new religion, but the conversion of the energies you carry into light. **This very "suffering" is the raw material out of which God's Light and God's Love are forged. When you are standing ON the Cross, rather than under it, you have accepted that truth.** It is only when you forget this or do not allow yourself to know, that you simply suffer.*

My mind is going out. I can hardly stay with You.

*We are talking about Faith. That is the agent of transformation. You put one foot down and the next foot down and you keep walking no matter what. You are already doing it now. You are beginning to carry your Cross. You are not yet standing on it, and when that time comes, you will know and We will know. The **purpose** of the "issues" in your life is to provide the fertile ground in which the seeds of Soul-flowers can be planted **and bloom** through your vehicle.*

*Here is another way to understand the Cross. In the center of the Cross lies the seed of a particular incarnation. In the center is Soul but We call it a seed here for your better understanding. The Horizontal Plane is the place where the life experience of the personality emerges perfectly and completely from the seed in the center. The Vertical Plane, which is crossed with the Horizontal Plane, symbolizes the ascent to God **also inherent** in the seed at the center. **The Seed is YOUR PARTICULAR PART in God's Love. It is your particular part in God manifesting the Divine, perfectly and all-knowingly in every corner of the universe.** In the center of the Cross is your heart. It is where Horizontal Plane ego energy intersects with Vertical Plane* *soul energy. It is the place of intersection in the heart that forms the cross, and it is here that one awakens onto to road of Return. There is nothing to resist. There is only one direction. We are waiting and We are your arrow marker on the road.*

***

The emergence of Christ and the image of the Cross in the writing came so naturally and seamlessly that I did not feel any resistance to entering that realm. In fact, Their messages about Christ felt utterly transcendent, like an "Aha!" that reverberated in my soul. I had no associations whatsoever with the symbol of the Cross or knowledge of the man Jesus beyond the traditional lore. And yet, as this Christ energy opened itself to me, it felt like another doorway to Home.

At the very same time, I thought, oh no, I can't be talking about THIS.

Chapter VII

I had another spectacular day in terms of You and what is allowed to pass through me. I find I have an increasing desire to hear Indian chanting music from back in the Muktananda days. It's as if I need to take in a sound that matches what I feel inside. Yesterday I bought two tapes and put them in the Walkman while I worked out in the yard. What I felt was overwhelming. I hesitate to write it in here because again I feel like a crazy person. I felt Muktananda there even though I never considered him my teacher or had any particular interest in Siddha Yoga. But his presence was so powerful out there in the yard, he could have walked up to me and I would not have been surprised. I felt like I would explode if I couldn't chant, so I ran into the house and put on the stereo. I let sound come out of me in a way I can't ever remember doing. I could barely recognize my own voice, fear rising up that the kids would come home and hear me and think I had lost my mind. But I let it happen as much as I could.

Let me interject here that I never considered Muktananda my teacher. I went to the Ashram, as I said, in order not to be totally alienated from my husband's life. Nevertheless, I did love the chanting. But I never wanted to be a groupie, ever. I prized my lonely little individuality probably the way any misfit would rather have some distinction in their misfit-ness than be lost in a crowd of conformity. I'm not saying that was the only choice, but I think I saw it that way. And I had a horror of ritual of any kind, had no interest in learning anything about Siddha Yoga, was completely uninterested in meditation, and yet there I was anyway walking down those extremely long Darshan lines, laying mangoes and oranges at the feet of the guru, heart pounding in longing for recognition and some Divine touch despite myself.

I had a moment looking up at Muktananda from far back in the meditation hall when I felt a bolt of incredible electric energy shoot through me. Whatever it was, it was undeniable. But I have *never* liked those kinds of stories, and there were so many people telling them back then— about the Shakti and The Blue Pearl and Kundalini and Krias, people squawking like chickens in meditation and all that. I thought those stories were self-conscious, look-at-me, the-guru-loves-*me*-stories and even so, I judged myself as less-than by comparison. The guru always seemed to love someone else better, more. But I also saw my own longing to be special everywhere and it disgusted me. I know now it was all grist for the so-called mill, but back then, I was just ground up in it and not being baked into any sort of beautiful braided bread. And on top of all that, Bill had his affair with one of the women in the Satsang and so I was *really* burnt out on what Muktananda called the Play of Human Consciousness. If that was the Play, I didn't want to be in it.

I thought I was done with gurus. So it was a complete surprise when the energy of Muktananda came to me the way it did in 1995. And I only tell you this part of my story now because what that energy imparted to me cannot be left out, *not* because I am special, not because God somehow loved me more. I know now that God loves us all.

Up until now, you have believed that only the moments of felt connection are desirable, are progress– when your heart is filled with Us or when you see the Buddha or you have a flash of insight. This is incorrect, although We understand why you have seen it this way. You are in a place on the path where you are learning to make a clear distinction between what is from self and what is from Soul. But notice that every time you feel completely disconnected, you then have a new experience of Presence. You see, you are no less connected in this moment than you were yesterday. This is a dichotomy that you can now transform by seeing it not as Presence versus lack of Presence, but as direct Light on the Path you are following, on the one hand, and **the experience necessary on the Horizontal Plane** *to move further in that direction on the other. This is another way to see the Cross. Your work is focused on* **the INTERSECTION of Horizontal and Vertical Plane energies, on the intersection of Soul with ego.** *And this intersection of energies repeats itself over and over again as you learn to* **Undo** *all the places where ego energy blocks the light of soul from shining through.*

When you **carry** *the Cross, you are* **in the experience necessary to move you where you are going on your Path. When you stand on the Cross, you are there, awaiting further direction from God.** *This is a very rough translation and it will emerge further as We go. This is what transformation could begin to be about for you. This is what Jesus understood and what We meant when We told you that he was not suffering in his journey because he had already chosen it long before. He lived every step of his path in a state of conscious transformation. This is what it means to "pick up your own cross." You embrace every step of you path with as much consciousness and willingness as you are capable of, opening to learning in every moment without judgment of self or other as to what form Teacher takes.*

Suffering is a state of unconsciousness of the Path. Faith is the bridge that takes you from unconscious suffering to conscious participation in manifesting Soul through the form that is you. *There are other bridges—and We will share them with you.*

125

*Stop judging the state you are in as either more or less connected to Us. Focus your energy on **what is to be learned, what is to be transformed**. Listen for Us to come to you in all forms. Nothing is extraneous. Bless the moments when your heart is filled to overflowing. These are gifts of Love from God to you, to help you keep your Faith and point the way to the Divine. Bless also the moments of darkness and confusion. These are gifts of Food you are to consume and transform according to God's Purpose in the Universe.*

Unable to sleep. Quite another incredible day. What I wrote this A.M. was tremendous. I see that I either feel especially awful or especially special. But can I just be so grateful and amazed at what I am receiving from You without having to worry that I am somehow in my ego over it all?

*Yes. There is a difference between seeing yourself as personally taking credit for what you have been given, and simply **taking joy** in what you have participated in creating through the vehicle that is you. You are too quick to judge your experience negatively, not that that is anything new! Take great joy in what is happening to you. God wants to be experienced with great love and joy, the love and joy God has. It is not all suffering. Bow to that. Kiss the feet of the Creator with that in your heart. When you know you are allowed joy, your feet are on the Road Home. You are allowed to feel joy when the Kingdom of Heaven opens its doors to you.*

Chapter VIII

I must learn what it means in my Path that I crash after every deep connection. The more I get in touch with my truth, the more this core fear is activated. *Every time.* Before, I only related that to my childhood in this life. It just can't be denied any longer that this terror goes back before this lifetime. I just know that I was *killed* for speaking, for following my Way, and the deeper I go, the more this fear is unearthed, *viscerally, in my body.*

I had a vision. I don't know what it was really. But I was remembering the bedroom I slept in with my sister growing up. I saw myself as a little girl on my bed and then suddenly the little girl was gone and on the bed, I saw a pile of ashes.

*The larger point is to understand that **there is a theme that has followed you through many incarnations**. And as We have said, you have the opportunity to complete the work of many lifetimes in this round. Therefore, you must now face the fear of persecution, of extinction and annihilation, and **SPEAK ANYWAY**. This time you have the opportunity to speak your truth **with the conscious recognition that you have chosen this**, just as We spoke about Christ. You **choose** now to walk every aspect of this Path with consciousness and love of God, bearing all your gifts and placing them at the feet of the Creator with love. This is what you do. In this way, you will come to **stand** on your Cross.*

*You will flip flop from ecstasy to despair and back again until you pick this piece up with consciousness and walk with it. You have the opportunity to face your fear by looking at the whole picture as We are showing it to you and seeing the essence. You, **just as you are,** with*

Phyllis E. Leavitt M.A.

whatever "issues" you carry, are a vehicle of God. We, Soul, are a vehicle of God's experience of the Divine. Your "issues" are the vehicles of your experience of yourself. That is what matters. Meditate on yourself, always and in everything.

The desire to chant is still very great. In a funny way, it is a similar experience to when I had body memories. It feels like another person inside me having these experiences, totally outside the realm of any conscious choice. It feels like it chose me. I think I understand the bigger picture, that **the panic is my teacher, that *everything* is my teacher,** that if I want to really transform my life, I have to look at everything in it as my teacher.

*There are several aspects to the anxiety and fear. One is that it is a way to let you know your memories are real. Do not doubt anything. Do not turn aside from any teacher that presents itself to you. It is as simple as that. **Your only choice is to choose what has already been chosen for you and by you.** Secondly, Teacher comes in many forms, just as We showed you earlier that love comes in many forms. What you think of as mundane is as holy as what you now think of as spiritual. The third aspect of the panic is that We love you and do not want you for a moment to sleep in unconsciousness. This you might say is your crown of thorns—for now. This has been given to you to speed you on your way Home. Accept this gift.*

Last night chanting– I heard You say that everyone has this knowing– every creature is born with this knowing inside them, that it is inherent in the soul of every being, that we are all incarnations of God. That animals, plants, and inanimate objects like rocks also have this knowing. It is not something a person acquires but something they come into life with. And it brought me back to what You told me in the beginning, that You are me.

*And you heard the next step, which is to **speak** your truth. That is the Act of Faith that is asked for. It is an **action of faith** that is required, not just a feeling or a focus of thought. **The action is transformative**.*

This is most definitely a part of your Path. You heard that there is a pattern that is very old in your spirit's path of descent and ascent that has to do with living your truth in secrecy and facing the fear of death and destruction if you were found out or if you spoke out. You are asked to speak out once again, for many reasons. With your voice, you redeem the Scream. Your voice will teach you. You are asked to speak. This writing is only one level. It is a first level. It is your Teacher on paper. There are other Teachers. Inside your Temple, you are to bow down to them all. Though you do not yet know them, they will make themselves known to you when the time comes. The serpent will uncoil inside you and you are not allowed to stop it.

I can see that it is because I *don't* talk about my deepest reality that the split is so bad. I have been hiding the biggest part of myself all my life. It seems like a revelation of the obvious. *This is who I am.* There is no one else and nothing else to work with.

*The worst thing of all, worse than all the abuse, is the fear of oneself, the loss of oneself, the estrangement from oneself, and the hatred of oneself. There is nothing worse than the wilderness you already have experienced because it is estrangement from one's own soul. When you **agree** to be with yourself everywhere, when you agree to see yourself exactly as you are, completely and in all aspects, in all feeling states, in all body states, in all mental states as well as in all spiritual states, then you will know what happened and you will know what is to happen next. You will read the book of yourself. But you see, you already know.*

*A "spiritual state," a state of being connected to Soul, to Us, to God, a state of feeling Love in your heart or a flash of recognition that comes out of the mind of God– **is not an end in itself** as so many seekers along the way mistakenly think. Having a "spiritual experience" (or a practice) opens a **possibility** of transformation just like learning the alphabet opens the possibility of language, or learning the scales opens the possibility of music. **Spirituality is not a prescribed state of being that is the same for all individuals. Spirituality is the work of*** *finding your Path, of accepting it when you find it, and the Faith to follow where it takes you. On higher and higher, more and more Light-filled, Love-filled rounds of the spiral it goes. Another way to say it is that spirituality is the work of finding God and Soul, accepting God and Soul exactly as you find them, and following the direction they point no matter what. At any one time in a given person's life, their spiritual "attainment" can be no more than the sum total of all the other aspects of their existence. When a person experiences moments of intense connection to Soul and to God, it has nothing to do with the person's worth or his so-called level of development. It has only to do with the Infinite power of God's Infinite Love. That person is blessed with the light of God calling him or her Home, but that person still has to make the journey.*

Your life, EXACTLY as it is, IS THE PATH YOU ARE ON. THIS is the only path to follow. THIS is the only path that will take you where your soul is longing to go.

*It is **not** about worthiness. Every atom of the manifest universe is worthy because it **IS**. Therefore, every aspect of your life is spiritual, and that is why We tell you to worship yourself, bow down to yourself, see your Teacher as yourself. Love even the darkness as much as you love the light. God in essence does not make that distinction. The man in the car cannot hurt you, your parents cannot hurt you, and your ex-husband cannot hurt you. Your own thoughts cannot hurt you. UNLESS YOU BELIEVE THEY ARE MORE POWERFUL THAN GOD IN YOU. WHEN YOU BOW DOWN TO YOURSELF AND TO THE TEACHER IN THE HEART, FOR THAT IS WHERE YOUR TEACHER DWELLS, WHEN YOU BOW DOWN TO YOURSELF, NOTHING CAN HURT YOU. SOUL IS INVINCIBLE.*

*Phyllis, We are always here. Will you come to Us completely? How long will you hang over this fence fearing the crossover to the other side? Let everything that unfolds unfold, like your writing last night. Was it not one more step in the **Revelation of yourself as the Way**? If each atom of the created universe allowed itself to know what it truly* *knows, this cycle of creation would come to an end and move on to another beginning. If you will but allow yourself to know what you already know, you need nothing else in this lifetime. Is the power of that statement clear to you? In Faith, say yes to the knowing that is in you. Say yes to the voice that longs to speak. Do not fear pain. Pain is nothing. Pain is everything to you humans and it is also nothing. Your voice is your Teacher. Has that teacher not been present in every word of poetry you wrote, in every line of your thesis, in every word you speak to clients, to your children, to your friends, in every word We write through you?*

*You need only realize Soul is there, speaking to you, calling to you. Drop your judgment of good and bad, kind and unkind, right and wrong. Drop your judgment and **listen**. Don't ask what **should** come out of your mouth– listen to what **does** come out of your mouth. Don't ask what you **should** do– learn from what you actually do. Don't ask what you **should** feel– learn from what you do feel. Keep reading the book of yourself. Keep reciting the story of yourself. This is your Way. This is your only Way. Say yes to your Way with your whole heart. All else is fruitless and illusion.*

I am sitting here at my computer and it is seven-thirty in the morning. After I got up I heard You say that I must bow down to myself and not resist anymore, not try to be a different person or have a different path. I feel so grateful for that because every time I go away from what comes up inside me, I am lost.

*You are not lost but found. That does not mean that your test of faith will not meet you at every turn in the road. Expect it. Know it for what it is, as the **fire** that burns away all that keeps you from going Home. Nothing more. Expect it, honor it, love it and bow down to it in your heart, in your Soul. You are afraid to live in your Soul, yet nothing will bring you more joy, more happiness, more of the deep connection you crave. Do you see the picture We show you, you standing on a bed of flames? Do you see that you are whole, un-charred, that your head is high though your feet are buried in the fire?*

We are here to tell you that your true nature is loved by God. Just write exactly what We tell you.

I have to ask myself over and over again, "What if all my memories are true? Everything in me says they are. My whole life is a testimony to the truth of them. My Soul is a testimony of the truth of them. Dear God, please let me lay down my resistance. Let me do what You were talking about the other day when You said that if every atom of the created universe allowed itself to know what it truly knows, this cycle of creation would end, and a new round would begin. I would like that to be me, that I could allow myself to know what I truly know, to accept it, and speak it.

Chanted and meditated tonight. I see Muktananda all around me. Saw him standing over me and then it was as if he came and sat in the lotus position in my heart and in my head. I saw the Buddha, palms together over his head making a Temple of his body. I asked him to be my Teacher. I said I want to learn and there was subtle golden light again in my head. I think I am beginning to understand that I am the Way.

I let my voice just pour out of me. I remembered the time last December when God came to me with such unearthly Light and vibration of Love in my heart. And then I felt Muktananda *showed me* that God had come just in the moment when I was in the deepest pain of my memories. **THAT** was the moment God came, **THAT** moment, when I was in the black hole of abuse. Then the golden light in my forehead came back and I heard a voice that said, "Isn't it interesting, Phyllis, that this golden light came last time when you were talking about abuse and now it comes again at the very same kind of moment. This is no mistake." I felt this giant male presence saying, *This is the truth. We have come to back up the truth of your memories.* Though it felt like a male presence, it was something much bigger than a man. It was a male force but not a male human. It had a Staff and said, *I am your Staff. I am the right hand of God.* I let myself hold the awareness that *everything is true.* I found myself crying.

I went to a talk by a well-known spiritual teacher.

(The talk) brought back all my black sheep feelings, and yet I can no longer discount myself the way I once did. She talked exclusively about being happy, about not letting yourself be run by your bad feelings or your shadow. She said there is no place for tears except for the tears of gratitude. This is NOT where I am. I believe now that there is a place for ALL the tears. I feel I really know something for myself now. I have a road to follow. I have something to come back to in myself that is unshakable, that's true for me. Every day I am more and more aware of what a great gift I have been given.

*Yes, it is true. No matter what comes your way, you have a place inside you, forged out of the years of your work on this earthly plane and in this earthly body, that can digest the food of your own experience, and **everything is food**. Remember, Phyllis, that everything you experience, inside and out, is your Teacher. A Guru is the outer manifestation of that. The true Guru is not a form, not a doctrine, not a course, a lesson, or even a body. "Guru" is the conductor of the energy of Teacher in the highest sense of the word and does not appear the same to all who see a body or have an experience that contains this energy. Thank the Teacher in you for what you learned today. There is nothing higher, better, or truer out there. Worship yourself, bow down to yourself, light the candle within you and let it shine within you and let that candle light your way. Bow down to the talk you heard, as it strengthened your adherence to the Path you travel. You will learn, **with people**, what it means to hold your center outside the realm of the personal life you have created. You will burn up what you no longer need. Bow down to that. Love that. When you see Soul in all things, then you will see there is no right and there is no wrong and there is no good or bad, there is **only Teacher** everywhere. You devour your experience. You eat it.*

Over and over again, the message was the same—There is no way around but *through*. The greatest teacher is one's own self, one's own experience, and the learning that soul seeks comes through embracing every aspect of what we find and what we face within ourselves and in the outside world. It seemed so simple, but it wasn't easy. I had been running from who I perceived myself to be and what I felt about myself for my whole life. I wanted to be anyone but me. Coming home to myself, just as I was, seemed like the most difficult task of all.

Chapter IX

And so, no sooner spoken than one of the greatest teachers ever presented to me was there, helping me from the soul side learn what I came to learn. I did not have the ability at that time to sit calmly in the eye of that storm contemplating "Teacher." Teacher hasn't worked that way in my life and I don't know if it ever will. Teacher seems to whip up the sands of my evolutionary path into a blinding storm so that I am pushed way beyond my known limits to finally see through it with totally different eyes.

Izzi (my daughter) is home and I am really having a hard time holding onto a sense of myself around her.

Do not underestimate the power of this relationship or of this Soul. Together you have chosen a very powerful interaction in this life. Drop your desire to see that relationship through the eyes of a traditional (whatever that is!) mother-child relationship. Drop your need to have your children reflect your worth. That very old unconscious form will not serve you. You still believe that if your child "fails" at something, it is a reflection of your inadequacies as a mother. You still believe that everything around you has the potential to undress you in public and reveal your shame. It is only on the surface level that Izzi is a reflection of you. The work with her is part of your Supreme Path, bigger than you now know.

*The task, Phyllis, is not to "save" her from pain. Believe Us when We say how deeply We know and understand that impulse in you. Your Path is to separate yourself from your children at this level of interaction and connection. They did not come here to be rescued by you. No one came here to be rescued by anyone. **People come into each other's lives to present them with opportunities for growth.** That is all. Even if you save a man from a fire, that does not mean you came here to save him or that he came here to be saved by you. You came together in that instant to learn from each other, to experience a particular aspect of your existence in the same place at the same time. **You are manifestations of Teacher for each other**. This does not mean you are not supposed to feel your motherly impulse of protection and deep love, bonding and involvement with your children. Not at all. That is supremely why Izzi has incarnated as your daughter rather than as a client or friend. You are here together in exactly the roles you are intended to be in. What could be simpler or more profound?*

*When you live in Soul in relation to her, you will see her Soul purely shining, lighting her way, and your shadow will not fall across her Path. You are still obsessed with what you do or did that you judge as right or wrong. Do you how **Karma** is created? When you cast your shadow or project your ego energy onto another and they absorb that energy, you have created something that is a confusion of your two energies that eventually will have to be untangled. When you live in Soul, when you even strive to live in Soul, you keep your shadow and your projected energy more and more to yourself. You take back into yourself and work out with God what is to be worked out for **your Redemption, not for another's**. This means you hold to your own truth and you act as much as possible from the direction of your own soul's guidance, no matter who you are relating to. On the Path of Return, it **is the power of your own inner work, the voice of soul in YOU,** which you bring to another, not what you think they need. This is how you undo Karma.*

This is where so many religions go so sadly off course. This is why it is so very difficult to be a true Teacher in this world. A true Teacher keeps a perfect balance between radiating every bit of light his Soul *seeks to emit in whatever ways his Soul seeks to shine AND he worships with **equal** devotion the Soul in all life forms he encounters. A true Teacher does not "save" anyone. **A true Teacher touches the wick of your candle with his flame because his own soul asked him to shine his light for the highest good of ALL. IF you accept it, your own candle will burn within YOU.** And then that Teacher's part in your play and your part in his are complete. In too many religious and spiritual paths, the one calling himself "teacher" falls prey to the desire to stay "teacher" forever, to become the "savior" of souls, and likewise too many devotees believe they can only be "saved" by agreeing to be "sinners," or those in a one-down role.*

*The concept of taking back projected energies is very critical to all Soul development. It is what We call the work of **Redemption**. You are taking back all the ego energies you have put out on the Horizontal Plane over lifetimes and you are giving back all the projected ego energies from others that you have absorbed. You are converting all the energies you take back into pure energy for use by your soul for the highest good of all.*

(The work of Redemption is further explained as the writing continues. An actual practice of how to work with the energies we carry in our ego consciousness, how to "take back our projections," how to begin the process of "unsticking" from the Horizontal Plane and make the energy of our personality available to soul, will be explained in much greater detail. They call this the Path of Supreme Surrender and there is a meditation called The Breath of the Cross Meditation that outlines the beginning of this work. But again, these explanations unfold over time. Here at the beginning, the groundwork is being laid.)

Whenever you believe you are responsible for another's progress, you have strayed from this road. You give what Soul in you seeks to give and you let go as soon as it is released from you. At the very same time, you worship every atom of this manifest universe as the holiest presence of the living God, without distinction and without judgment. Do this twenty-four hours a day and you will be a realized being.

*Your daughter is **Teacher** in one of its infinite forms. Who tells the Teacher what to teach?*

*Do not think about what you are supposed to do. Do not think about what a "good mother" does even, although you are free to think about that, of course. We are saying look into **your Soul** for guidance, follow that guidance without fail and you will learn what your experience is here to teach **you**. If you do this with Izzi, you will know clearly what to do and say. It is the same with everyone. Then you do not run the risk of focusing on judgment of others. You do what it is in you to do. Your "success" is not dependent on the other's response in any way. "Success," if you want to use that word, is following the voice of soul regardless of the apparent outcome on the Horizontal Plane.*

*You will then see that taking your stand, sharing with your daughter the greatest light you are capable of, is just the first step. **The next step is to digest her response (to digest all responses from others), use the nutrients in it, grow from that food, and repeat this process again and again.** It doesn't matter what the response of the other is. It **doesn't matter** if you consider it positive or negative. It is ALL Teacher in its essence. In this case, you accept your role as parent and the responsibilities inherent in that role on the ordinary life plane, however you understand them, and you go this step beyond toward the unflagging development of your own soul consciousness. As you digest ALL food that is offered you in ALL experiences and as you power the engine of soul with that energy, your light increases and you become of greater and greater Service in the world.*

When you are talking about parent/child relationships, this is extremely difficult to do. The bond on the Horizontal Plane is very deep and very strong. But the intensity of that bond is exactly what makes it such an abundant and powerful source of energy for the growth of soul consciousness. This is why humans were created as child-bearers of small numbers of live, dependent young. There is a **Soul purpose** *for the bonds, requirements, and developmental processes of family relationships, which is rarely grasped. Family relationships are special relationships, not to be judged as good or bad. Family groups are groups of mutually incarnating Teachers for each other. You could say they are sub-groupings of Souls, as in a class where the students are assigned to small groups to work on specific projects. One of the reasons why modern civilization is in such a mess is that this understanding of family has been lost and people spend lifetimes* **fleeing** *the lessons or challenges they were born into only to find themselves attaching to other people who offer the very same challenges. Without the concept of the Purpose of Family, the significance of this process is lost, often for lifetimes, usually until great crisis or pain or Grace makes it clear. This very understanding is something that modern psychology is beginning to approach, and when the psychology of the family can be formulated with the perspective of* **the growth of soul consciousness as its purpose**, *the gap between psychology and spirituality will begin to close.*

Nothing is an accident.

I am so grateful– I want to say it again– for everything that is coming through in this writing. Maybe You can help me with my fear, not only for Izzi's safety and survival and my role in relation to that, but also for my fear of her anger.

Actually, Phyllis, **holding your ground against another's anger is exactly what you have been seeking in this experience.** *That is why sometimes from Our side it is either very funny or very tragic to watch as people struggle and resist with all their might the very experiences they took form to redeem. When you reach a snag or an overwhelming block in your life, in that very experience* **Soul is bringing you face to face with the purpose of your incarnation.** *So you see, just as you have been learning to bow down to whatever manifests* **inside** *you,*

139

whatever you feel or think or sense, in the very same way you also bow down to whatever your world offers you.

The Teacher within and the Teacher without are one and the same.

*Has it occurred to you that anger has been one of your greatest hurdles to overcome? You took a breath outside after an angry exchange with your son just now, and you told yourself that you could be with what you were feeling. You didn't lapse into self-blame. This is a step in what you came to do. You are **Undoing** an age-old pattern. Do you see that up until now, on an unconscious level, you have equated standing up for yourself with either hurting another or with life-threatening danger to yourself? Do you see that you can move past that now?*

Your words hit me like revelations. I am so grateful for Your presence. I believe You when you say that these stuck places or difficult issues are exactly what I came here to deal with. That nothing is an accident; nothing is even "bad."

Yes. That is why We call to you so loudly. Because your time has come.

*There are lessons here in the very challenges you face on a daily basis that are not available anywhere else now. Ultimately, the messages you receive from Us are only useful, only truly valuable, if you **apply** everything you receive. This is the time to do it. There are bridges that can be crossed in only this way. It is so simple really. **You are EXACTLY who you were intended to be. You meet in life EXACTLY what you are intended to work with—people, situations and issues. You need these life experiences to find Soul.** There is further understanding of this not yet available to you. APPLY everything We have outlined. Nothing is more important. In fact, nothing else really matters. What We tell you is a light that is intended to shine, first and foremost, into your dark places. If it does not shine there, before all else, you have missed the mark. Do you see what has been entrusted to you?*

I began to see a larger picture behind my own struggles. If I personally was exactly who I was intended to be, if I was meeting in life exactly what I came to work with to find soul, then it would follow that we all—individually, as families, nationally, ethnically, globally—are also who we are intended to be, facing the challenges we intended to face to create consciousness of soul on earth. If my biggest challenges were my greatest teachers, then it would also follow that our biggest challenges as a human race are our greatest teachers. The picture was so big. I couldn't stay there because of the intensity of what I was experiencing on my own small scale, but the scope of what They were saying was not lost on me.

Wanting to be with You this morning but feeling I have already received more than anyone has a right to ask for. I go into a fog so quickly and I have a hard time coming out.

Never hesitate to call on Us. We do not sit here and judge you and your accomplishments. We do not say, Sorry, you are not good enough today, come back tomorrow after you have become more worthy. You are still too harsh a critic of yourself. Our point, Our purpose, is to help you Push Through. You do not do that by beating yourself up. Will you hear this? Will you love yourself today as We love you? Every time you look toward the light, every time you take the tiniest step toward the light, the Love of God surrounds you with a special presence. The Love of God always surrounds you, always surrounds, infuses, and informs everyone, every atom, and every creature of the created Universe.

*Do you honestly believe that the difficulties you experience with your children, your parents and your memories are so because of your **failings** and deficiencies? You see, We know that you **do** believe that and We are here to tell you that that is not true. You are blessed in all things. You are given tremendous challenges because **on a Soul level*** *you asked for them. It is not difficult because you are deficient. It is difficult because that difficulty brings you the greatest opportunity, the greatest possible Soul food on the earth plane.*

Could this really be true for the human race? With all the suffering, injustice, cruelty and pain in the world, this idea was difficult to fathom. If my struggles were not a sign of my deficiencies or unworthiness, then the problems of the human race could not be a sign of original sin or failure either. How could I begin to understand that as a race we also asked for the very challenges we face?

*Know that what you feel inside yourself as fear of speaking, fear of ridicule, fear of being not being heard, fear of being wrong, fear of not being believed, and ultimately fear of destruction – the fear you feel inside is **the accumulated Karma of your particular Path. That is the dark shadow of projected energy that you have absorbed over time that you came here this round to dispel.** And you think that should be an easy task? That if it is difficult for you then you are a meaningless failure? It cannot be other than extraordinarily difficult! That is where Divine Love comes in. Think about that. There is nothing that reflects back to you an overwhelming feeling of failure and inadequacy but you. Live your day. Let the Love inherent in ALL THINGS speak to you, hold you, help you on your Way. Hold Us in your heart and in your mind and in your essence. You are on the Road of Return.*

If my personal difficulties were the accumulated Karma of *my* path, then *our* difficulties had to be the accumulated Karma of *OUR* PATH. What was our path? These questions were daunting to say the least, but they were in the background at that time. My own issues were too overwhelming. My personal teacher, in the form of my daughter, was all I could contend with.

Chapter X

So let me fill you in about my beautiful Isabella, my middle child. There was always something about her. Everyone noticed her, commented on her beauty, her intelligence, and her creativity. She was the one who was unbelievably content as a baby, who could entertain herself with her own imagination for hours on end. She thrived in school. She seemed to have the Leavitt brain as we called it. Her fourth grade teacher told me in all his years of teaching he had never had a student as bright as Izzi.

Back when the kids were little, I was like one watching a train wreck in slow motion, my ineffective cries swallowed up in the roar of what was coming down the tracks. I tried to compensate for the deficiencies in my marriage and our family life by reading endless stories, sewing clothes, trying new recipes, but I couldn't compensate for what was missing. It wasn't just an involved father that was missing. It was also a powerful mother. If I had *really* stood up for my children I would have left the marriage long before I finally did. But instead, my children went on hurting. Eddie showed it openly. Izzi, on the other hand, almost never let anyone see her feelings and even when I knew she was upset, she would not tell me what was bothering her. She seemed to manage it all internally on her own. She seemed happy, incredibly "well-adjusted," through the worst of it. When Bill and I told the kids we were getting divorced, Izzi didn't cry. She went into her room and wrote up a divorce decree complete with custody arrangements. I worried about Eddie. I never worried about her.

Adolescence hit them both early. We were in Santa Fe by then. I was in graduate school, writing papers, and reading books on Psychopathology and Family Systems Theory. I could not avoid the painful truth that unhealthy family dynamics were playing out in my own living room. I wondered if Bill was Bipolar as well as alcoholic. I *knew* I was an enabler. My friend D told Bill I would leave him as soon as I had my degree. *I* didn't even know that yet, but D was right.

In junior high, both Eddie and Izzi became part of a group, something I never had at that age. I was happy they had friends over and seemed to have a sense of belonging. I was so consumed by divorce and single parenting and my own unstoppable descent into darkness that I just went on doing the laundry when I smelled cigarettes in the garage one day. I didn't *really* smell cigarettes...did I?

The truth was that every new shred of evidence that my kids were going down the wrong road only immobilized me further, only reinforced the fact that I was a failure at the only job I had ever really wanted, which was to be a mother. The instinct to growl fiercely and protect at all costs should have sounded like a fire alarm inside me, but it didn't. I *felt* that instinct to protect, but I just couldn't *access* it. And I failed altogether to notice they were smoking pot in their rooms. I know it sounds unbelievable, but I didn't know what pot smelled like, and I guess I believed them when they said it was incense. I honestly don't remember at all.

I don't know exactly when Izzi started drinking more alcohol than your average teenager. I don't know when she started using drugs, but it was early on. Eddie, I guess, stuck with pot. Izzi, on the other hand, had nothing inside her that said no to any drug that came her way. I don't know if it was all about the pain she had never allowed herself to feel or if she inherited the tendency toward addiction or both, but she was full-on using like no one in either Bill's or my family and in treatment for the first time by the age of 15.

I was *completely* unprepared. And I mean completely. Not that that is an excuse for being unable to see what was right in front of me— the caustic defiance, the dilated pupils, the see-through lies, and the light gone out of my baby's star-studded sky.

It was all too much. You have to understand I came from a family of *good* kids who cleaned their rooms, did their homework and got as many A's as you could fit on a report card. We didn't have curfews, were never grounded, drunk or snuck out at night. I had *no* experience with setting limits.

You have to remember, too, that the family I came from had zero capacity to identify or address problems of any kind. My parents must have looked at me at some point and seen *something* that indicated all was not right, but they could not admit it or talk about it or even entertain the possibility. Sadly, I was not very different with my children. The lost look of my Eddie hanging onto friends who gave me the creeps, his drifting, pot-filled, unmotivated barely-hanging-on-in-school existence — *everything*, all the signs and symptoms were there. And my little cigarette –and-God-knows-what-else-smoking Izzi who got endless stares now not for her beauty but for shaved patches on the sides of her head and the nail-studded black leather jacket she wore even in summertime... I sank back into that undistinguished paralysis I knew so well.

It was totally out of my known world to have to put her in treatment. I'm not even sure how I summoned the will to do it. But she seemed to come around after she got out, even though she didn't go back to High School. I thought the worst was over. She started selling Mary Kay and all the black leather and torn pants went into the trash. Eventually, she applied to a drama school in L.A. and was accepted. I was so proud of her. I thought the worst was over. I thought she went to L.A. sober.

And, I literally had no idea the depth of Izzi's drug problem. I wish now that before she had been released from the hospital, someone had sat me down and told me straight out the morbidity rate for the disease *I had contracted along with her,* the disease that of course I had had for years. I wish someone had shoved a treatise about the risks and signs of relapse down my frigging throat. I wish they had shot me up with an anti-enabling/anti-denial serum, super-strength, shot me up until my arms ached and my veins stung. I wish they could have shot me up against that vicious virus, that insidious disease that walks in your door in the guise of your sweet little daughter, just hitting puberty, a few pimples breaking her innocent skin. Who would know to shut the door? Who could do it anyway? I wish just one person had told me how bad benzos and painkillers are. I wish now that they had screamed at me in some mothers-of drugs-addicts boot camp and made me do push-ups over little pill bottles and photographs of empty, dilated eyes. But I don't blame anyone. I was an educated, intelligent woman. I was a therapist, after all. Maybe they thought I knew. Maybe they, too, thought the worst was over.

I thought my beautiful Isabella would pick up where she had left off. It was just a bad phase. She'll grow out of it. She's half Leavitt and Leavitts aren't like this. No matter that she refused to go to high school. At least she shaved off the Mohawk that had been dyed red, yellow and puke, and I could see the beautiful shiny black roots growing in. And gone too were the black lines she penciled from the corners of her eyes into her hairline and the spiked necklaces and the nail earrings. Those were all good signs. Never mind she had dropped out of school and was selling beauty products. So it was unconventional, so it left her brilliant mind a wasteland for God knows what kind of

147

mutant seeds to take root, so what that she seemed to hang out with people 20 years older than herself whose IQ was half of hers, so what? Her beautiful dark hair was growing back. That had to count for something.

And I was already a master at putting square pegs into round holes in my mind because they just have to fit. Not really, but just enough so that I could get up in the morning, make coffee and talk like a "normal" person. Walking one step at a time over life, like an idiot on a high wire suspended over the Grand Canyon. You just focus every possible bit of psychic energy on taking that next step and that is all. That was me, and I'm so unbelievably afraid of heights! How the hell did I get out there?

I didn't have a clue. I was just *in it* with her back then. Her needs, her fears, her desperation, her failures all set off that inaudible alarm system in my psyche, just below the level of conscious hearing, and I would write a check to cover whatever the latest mishap was, the latest sign that the universe wasn't on her side and only I could save her– all the while telling myself some altered version of the truth. And of course, I had help; I think Izzi told me many altered versions of the truth. The job in L.A. where she was drug tested and not allowed to work while they waited for the results. That was random; she said. The roommate who said Izzi stole her clothes and then proceeded to steal Izzi's money. The restaurant job she lost before it began because she went into the men's restroom. The bad checks she wrote, the bills she never even tried to pay. The list is very long and I can't remember it all now. What did I tell myself? It was all some version of, Poor Izzi; nothing seems to go right for her.

All the alarms were going off and I was paying out more and more money to keep from hearing them. That is how the mother of an addict becomes sick, how the mother of an addict's perception of reality gets warped and skewed without her ever needing to ingest a single mind altering drug. Addiction alters *everybody's* mind. If you love an addict and you don't get a hell of a lot of help *right away, every day*, you might as well kiss your sanity, intuition, common sense, and vitality goodbye. I kissed mine goodbye when Izzi was 14.

Well, I had probably kissed it goodbye long before that, as you know.

The severity of her drug problem only really began to dawn on me when she came home for Thanksgiving her first year in L.A. She was 18. Her face was bloated, her eyes were funny, and that was the first time I heard the slur in her voice. She insisted that she was taking only the prescribed dose of Clonopin, an anti-anxiety medication. She insisted that her voice was normal, that she was just tired. And I *argued* with her, tried to get her to *agree* with me that there was something wrong. That tells you just how little I understood addiction at that point. I was arguing with her while her tongue was hanging out of her mouth. Not really, but you know what I mean.

You might ask why *I* didn't get help, right then, every day, why Al-Anon wasn't at the top of my list of priorities, why *I* wasn't doing massive therapy of my own. I'm a therapist, for God's sake. Well, I have that question, too. Near as I can tell you, the reason I didn't was that I truly believed that because *it was not supposed to be that way, it would get better.* I just had to hang in there, believe in her and help her, maybe pay a little more till she was on her feet, and she would somehow transform herself back into the radiantly exquisite child I knew and adored who was here just a minute ago, I swear. Surely, she would transform herself back into the little girl she had always been, that consummately feminine, self-expressed, dynamic little creature who lit up every room and lit up my frozen female like a million stars in a moonless sky.

I didn't get help because it was just a phase, because Jews are not addicts, because good mothers don't have addicted children...and because I was so ashamed.

She went in and out of sobriety for several years. And it was during those same years that I did my most intense inner descent and finally found this most precious inner voice. During that time, I lived on the roller coaster of her drug use—from hope to despair and back again. Don't get me wrong. I didn't do *nothing.* I tried talking to her again and again, wrote her letters reminding her of her essential beauty and worth, like the letters Bill Moyers wrote to his son Cope when he was on crack. I cried with her, begged her. We did a family intervention. Eddie, who had long since gotten his life together, whose stunning depth and radiance reappeared when the haze of pot smoke cleared, poured his heart out to her ironclad, curtains-drawn little soul to no avail. I did end up consulting addictions people. I did go to Al-Anon.

Nothing changed. Roller-coaster ride, stomach dropping out, and then up again readying for the next plunge into hell. It was in June of 1995 when Izzi's roommate called me not knowing where Izzi was. She had gone to pick her up at the airport and she wasn't on the plane (returning to L.A. from Santa Fe). I was beside myself with worry. My friends came over to be with me. Finally, Izzi called about 11:00 pm crying hysterically. She was in the Las Vegas airport, had gotten off at her layover, and had not been able to get back on the plane. She said she felt like she was losing her mind, that she needed to go to a psychiatrist for anti-depressants, and that she felt totally lost and didn't know what to do. I offered for her to fly back home but she didn't want to so I decided to go out and be with her in L.A.

I was by then newly into this writing and so I had a place to turn besides addictions counseling and Al-Anon, not that there was anything wrong with those avenues. But I needed something more.

I want to talk to You about it more than anything else right now. After I got over the initial hysteria, when I knew she was safe, then I could begin to breathe into the experience. This morning I could feel such a depth of meeting myself right here with her and so great a connection to my Teacher that I was filled with tears and an indescribable feeling. I am asking that You talk to me and help me.

151

*And you hear Us already telling you that this experience is Teacher expressing itself for you and for Izzi and it is given to you both with great Love. Remember that Teacher, Guardian and Guide of your Soul, does not come in any predictable form. **THIS is the dirt and stones of your real life. THIS is what you are surrendering to and transforming.** Look at all experience on the earth plane through this lens. What to do and what to say is in you and you will find it. For Izzi, it is about hitting a wall and what she is able to redeem at this time from the experience and what she is not able to redeem that she will redeem later, as her Path guides her. **Your job is to shine your light unwaveringly**, to stand in your truth, and shine your light with great love, which you are capable of doing. In that process, you will discover what your light is. And it is an ongoing, unending process of discovery. As yet, you do not know what your light is, nor will you ever fully know. This is a Great Truth for all on their Path. Your light shows you the next step on your path. It is the inspiration that keeps you walking. Then you reach the point where you must be willing to walk on without seeing the next step. When you keep trying to picture the landscape that awaits you around the bend in the road, you limit the view. **Your Karma is that you and Izzi meet with the force of your personalities in this shared experience. Your Soul Path is that you meet at this juncture as Souls, acting as teacher for each other in Undoing the energetic hold of your ego patterns on the Horizontal Plane.***

It seemed to be the same lesson, over and over—the lesson with M, with my parents, with daring to share the writing with other people—and now with my daughter. Again and again, soul asked me to stand in the fire of my truth and not be burned, to care in the earthly sense, of course, but to hold steady in my connection to my soul no matter what the response, and to know that this is not only what I came here to do, but that acting on the direction of soul is taking the first step on the Road Home. For me it always seemed to involve speaking what was most frightening to say. For others, it may be some other form of expression their souls wish to take. Again and again soul asked me to see that everyone in my life was playing exactly the part they came to play in relation to me—and to see *myself* as playing exactly the part I came to play in relation to them. With my parents, my children, my ex-husband, anyone– the point was not to judge right and wrong, good and bad. It was to discover what I was to *learn* and learn it.

*Do you see what We say? Your personality (your ego consciousness) is the Karmic aspect that brings you to this particular juncture at this particular time in this particular form. Your Soul is what brings you to the **Meaning** of it. Progress on the Path is moving to higher and higher levels of Meaning. Progress on the Path is not linear the way people ordinarily think it is. You do not go from A to B. You are always at A. And you RISE from there. You move onto the Vertical Plane from there. When you were wishing for something dramatic to happen in your daily life, some big change in circumstances to prove your progress, you were shown immediately that that is not the point. The Vertical Plane is **within** you.*

I loved what You said to me the last time about the process not being linear, that there is no A to B process, there is only A. It really helps me stay with the present moment. It also helps me focus more of myself internally and to stop looking for proof that I am okay.

And so it was perfectly true. I was at "A" and there was no possible "Z" to get to. Izzi's addiction was nowhere close to resolving back then. My role, both as her mother AND as a soul in relation to her soul, revolved around that "fixed" point. It's not really that her addiction per se was what I am calling A. "A" was our relationship as mother and daughter and Izzi's addiction was the focal point of our intersection at that time. I was learning to see the *meaning* of it in my life very differently. AND just as before, the pain of being her mother did not go away. That was clearly not the point. The point was to see that the darkness and pain of my ordinary life existence was the perfect doorway through which I was allowed to grasp the world of soul reaching down to me and lighting up all that otherwise would have been unbearable darkness. I would have been totally lost in the world of judging myself because I could not cure her disease, could not save her from pain. And most of all, I would have been totally lost in the fear of losing her, of her dying.

All pain is Soul calling you Home.

I told Izzi almost everything that has been in my heart to say for a very long time. She was very receptive. I understand that her receptivity was so great because her pain was so great and I just pray it will stay that way. It was incredible for me to finally be able to let out all this that has been bottled up in me for so long.

*You see that light is all around you. More exactly, the light is **in** you. When you look outside for "signs" of progress, you cannot see Light because Light does not reside there. **The Way** is the process of clearing out all blocks to seeing the light **within Yourself**. Therefore, We help you redirect your vision. All of life experience can help you redirect your vision. We know that you are afraid Izzi will not make it, that she will die from drugs, and We are saying that there **is** a dying taking place, but not of the body. Our message to you is that Dying is a Divine process; Death is a Divine state of being. Death, more exactly, is only a moment in the unending cycle of Creation of the Divine. Birth and Death are One. Dying truly is a cause for celebration. It is the* *celebration of the end of something that no longer needs to be. So little understood yet so profound.*

Remember the difference between Izzi's Soul Path and your own. Remember not only that they are different paths, but also that as they intersect according to the Divine intention inherent in Soul, you are to keep your sight most steadily on YOUR PATH, not hers. This is one of the great challenges of the Way, and it is especially great in relation to those you love the most or those who have the greatest influence in your life—whether you consider that influence "good" or "bad."

They gave me a reading for Izzi on her Soul Path and the big picture of the energies she came to work with. It was magnificent. It described all the light that was waiting to be redeemed from the depth of all the darkness she was carrying. I shared it with her. (And just so you know, she did not die, though she came very close, and everything They predicted about her path has unfolded.)

*However, what you share ends there in terms of what she does with what is given. That is up to her and her path. The focus for you is always on **your** path. Your Path does not culminate in the passing on of information. Remember this. The passing on of information is only a task you are given, or should We say, blessed with.*

All the sudden, after all these years of feeling lost, of feeling I was left by the wayside of life, I realize I am found.

I was at "A," and "A" was my life exactly as it was. I could live in the illusion that there was somewhere to run to on the Horizontal Plane, some way I could create a much prettier version of myself. *Or* I could try my very best to stay right where I was and swallow, digest and transform, the best I could, all that I had once considered poison– for the sake of my soul.

***

I'm in the airport on my way to L.A., looking at all the people and the TV blaring and wondering if it could really be true that we are ALL on a Path, ALL on our way Home, whether we know it or not. Not that I don't believe it when I am with You. But, I'm afraid to let You come here in the middle of all the noise of the airport.

We are everywhere. Television, people, and loud noises do not matter. There is NOWHERE inaccessible to Us, no moment, no feeling, and no situation. Don't limit yourself.

Here at Izzi's. She would rather not talk, which I get and I know it is part of my job to push through her resistance and my fear of her anger. I'm not as afraid as I have been. Listening to a chant with her. Realizing so strongly that the form and the power of Teacher are two different things and at the same time, there must be a piece of the Teacher in the form so that Teacher energy can be felt and sensed. Help me with Izzi today is what I ask.

We are here. The love of God is hovering, is present, all around the earth. Did you know that God never allows his creations to push him away? God waits forever, patiently, unconditionally, for all to hear and come. God is not, however, passive. No created entity can push the love of God away. It can resist, it can even fight and defy, but God's love is for everyone and everything and is eternal. There is no deed, no thought, no frame of mind or emotion that can push that love away.

You are in the same role with your daughter as God is with you. There is nothing she can do that will push your love away. We ask you to accept that more actively now. God is active.

Just as the suffering you experience with your daughter is for a purpose, the suffering on the earth at this time is also FOR A PURPOSE. Huge forces and energies are at work. You have been wondering if the perspectives you are being given are really the truth for the human race at this time. The answer is yes. Do not allow yourself to feel crazy because you stand in this space. This space is the road to freedom, freedom through PARTICIPATION in the Divine Plan. Do not allow your small self to be critical or skeptical. The more you FULLY EMBRACE what is being poured into your consciousness, the more you drink every drop, so to speak, the fuller and richer and more divine your life will become.

*You said that it felt as if another being was in you and you could feel it. Let Us clarify. What you felt was the presence of your own Soul. Your own Soul with the cloak of your sad-eyed, long-suffering little self pulled to the side, like the curtain of a stage is pulled open. When the curtain is closed, you cannot see the True Players and you can only guess at the Play. When it is open, you see the True Players and you see the Play as well. So what you felt is not someone else. It is you. You understand why the struggle with doubt is so important. Doubt keeps the curtain shut. Doubt says, "I'm crazy if I think there is anything more to me than little Phyllis Leavitt, scared and lonely." You are **not** little Phyllis Leavitt. You are a Divine Being. You are all Divine Beings. Remember this.*

You cannot consciously participate in the Divine Plan unless you can see it. You cannot see it until you see yourself. You Are The Way. The microcosm is the seed of the macrocosm. It is God in you and you in God. There is no spirituality apart from this very great Truth. Love yourself by staying in this Truth.

I feel totally up against it. Tried to talk again with Izzi and she was a wall.

Don't judge it. When you feel judgment come up in you about yourself— or anything else really— the idea is to look at it as Soul *pushing through in you to learn something, **not** to determine where you were deficient. You see how easily you can be silenced by another's silence? It feels dangerous to talk. You think another's lack of receptivity means you are doing something wrong and you will be rejected. **As you meet particular experiences along your Path, if you do not meet them with the full force of your Soul, then you meet them with the full force of your personality only**. This is not wrong. It is simply not what you are now seeking to create. It is this simple: you move from judgment of self and other to a focus on what there is to learn and transform **within yourself** in any given situation. This is shifting your awareness from the Horizontal to the Vertical Plane.*

*The creation of Karma– the wild play of projecting judgment, need, and power to influence, and the wild play of internalizing those ego energies– is **lawful** in the process of incarnation. However, as We have explained, Karma is created for the purpose of experience only and for the purpose of Soul Return ultimately. You are at the critical place on your Path, the center of the Cross, where your Soul's interest is no longer to **create** more Karmic experience but to **Redeem** it, take it back into yourself and convert it to pure energy for use by your soul. Therefore, on the Road of Return, as you move through the Horizontal Plane and its whirlwind of "illusions" about Reality, you will flip-flop back and forth between the whirlwind and the EYE of the storm. You will flip-flop between ego's perceptions and reactions and soul's vision and guidance. And, as you already see, your intent more and more is to move from the EYE, from soul, and not to be unconsciously hurling yourself about in the storm. This is what it means to move Vertically**, to leave the gravitational force** of the psyche. This is extremely difficult to do and yet you are capable of doing it because you ask to do it, you see to do it, and you long to do it. Therefore, yesterday is a perfect representation of the space in which you move. Now you brace yourself to stay in the EYE and you move from there as much as you can.*

***

I want to create a picture here that I think will clarify different concepts as they emerge. The image of the cross is created by the intersection of the Horizontal and Vertical Planes. The point of intersection holds the Soul Seed of the individual, which contains the entire "map" of their path through all their incarnations and their journey through ego consciousness, *as well as* the map of their particular Path of Return to Oneness. The Heart is at the center of the cross. In ego consciousness, we keep projecting our thoughts, feelings, actions and energies — lawfully — out onto the Horizontal Plane according to the pattern inherent in this map, according to the "part in the Play" each of us was asked and agreed to play on the Horizontal Plane AND invoking the reactive responses from others that make up the "play" we create together.

The continuous and increasingly complex process of **action and reaction** creates an extremely dense web of ego energy (Karma) that results in the Sleep of Forgetting of the Source from which we all came. And it is this Sleep of Forgetting, They said, that, on the Road Home, we help each other wake up from. The Road of Return is a road we walk *together*.

From what had been suggested to me about a connection to past lives and also what I had experienced in my present life, my particular "part" had something to do with having an awareness that was at odds with some prevailing point of view, whether it was in a group or my own family or the larger culture. I also understood that the specifics of any of these lifetimes were not as important as the *themes* I was playing out. In whatever "role" I took on, the responses of the outside world caused me to fear myself, abandon myself, silence myself or be silenced. This was the slowly emerging shape of my "part" on the Horizontal Plane. The dim outline of soul shining through all these forms was this– on the Road of Return I would have to speak out anyway and not abandon myself, no matter what.

As personalities, we come to believe in the parts we play until we enter the Road of Return. At that time, the work is to take back as much of our own projected ego energy as possible, not allow the projections coming at us to cloud our vision of ourselves as souls, begin to **understand the patterns we have been playing out**, and move into the center of the cross, into our Heart. This is what They call the work of Redemption — redeeming energy from the Horizontal Plane and giving it to soul. We intentionally begin to use the energy we are freeing from the Horizontal Plane to fuel our Vertical ascent — to illuminate soul in us and shine soul's light **in the world**.

This is what was being outlined for me in my experience with my daughter. The visual image of coming back into my heart, into the Soul Seed of my own existence and actively trying to convert the pain of my dynamic with Izzi and the fear of her dying into consciousness of my own soul was a point of light in the terrible darkness of that time. As her mother, I could not help wanting to "save" her. As a soul, I was trying to stay on my own path through the agony of what was happening with her on the Horizontal Plane, and return to my own heart again and again. As a soul, I was trying to Redeem all the energy still stuck in the very tight bond of our karmic relationship *while continuing to be her mother.* It wasn't an either/or. I didn't *go anywhere.* I was truly at "A." I *was* her mother, and I was being asked by soul to fuel my ascent to Oneness with the energy held in that bond. I was right in the center of the cross—I could keep the action/reaction pattern going ad infinitum or I could try to pull as much energy back into myself as humanly possible. I can't tell you how difficult that was, and yet there was *nothing else* to do.

***

Last night I began to see myself as less-than and I heard You come in immediately and say, *No, you are not little Phyllis Leavitt. You are a Divine Being.*

I saw years of intense negative self-judgment pass in front of my eyes and there was a lot of sadness there. I had to actively keep from turning it into self-criticism. I tell myself, So many wasted years. I struggle to hear Your voice that says—

Not wasted. All is exactly as it should be. Not wasted.

Hard for me to take it in totally, yet I must. I hear You say,

There is no time like the present. There is no time BUT the present. There literally is nothing else. There is no such thing as wasted time. It does not exist. When you put a seed in the ground, is the time wasted during which you cannot see the leaves unfolding from the kernel? If it snows and hails while still nothing pokes its head through the soil, is time wasted? Do you somehow imagine you know better than God the time frame and the steps in the germination process? Bow down to this in yourself and in all things.

Leaving L.A. today. Last night as I went to sleep, the vibration came twice in my forehead, with less color and more intensity of vibration. Then right after that, there was an intense blue burst of light in my head like a huge blue globe that exploded into hundreds of deep blue stars. My heart is overflowing. My form seems incapable of expressing the magnitude of what is happening. The chanting music has gone in and found my Soul and fills me with Love. God comes regardless of my state of being, regardless of my unending self-judgment. Let me take that in.

Chapter XI

B ack in Santa Fe and back to my ordinary life. Realize I have to bow down to everything, even the moments that seem not to contain much. Last night I chanted and felt Muktananda come and sit inside me. He showed me again that God dwells in each of us, and the more we know this, the more it will be impossible to hurt ourselves or hate ourselves or belittle others or ourselves.

But the fear of being presumptuous came up again. I was overcome with fear of being "found out," persecuted. I was surprised at how strong the feelings were, how intense the fear of the conservative aspects of our society. It has died down now. I feel ready to work with these things.

The more you see God in you, the less these feelings will control your behavior. See what you want to share, not necessarily what you think others will accept or be comfortable with. As with Izzi, stay with what is right for you to do and say. Meditate on it. Don't just leave it to chance. Remember that not owning your truth at all is one of the most self-destructive things you can do. At the very same time, bow down to the fear of speaking your truth.

Chanted last night before I went to bed. Nothing else is that interesting to me. I used to ask God to be of service in the world and as I said those same words last night, I realized that my request is now more to be living in my Soul, to be conscious of my Divine nature, to give myself to God and Soul and be *directed*. I am willing to not know what I am supposed to do or what will "happen" because I see now that what I do and what happens is not the central point. This is a difficult awareness to hold with the conditioning I have. The little girl in me still feels she has to prove herself to someone, feels she has to have something to show for herself. She still wants things.

*It is a mistake to look at your personality as something you want to get rid of or leave behind or to hope it will have no more influence on you. That is not the point at this stage. It is how you **use** the energies of the personality or ego that matters here. Look at your personality and your child-like parts as the yolk of your particular egg, as the **food** that nourishes and sustains you until the egg is ready to hatch. At that point, something different emerges. Something is growing and changing within the egg now and it is not up to you to determine when all the yolk has been absorbed and the shell is ready to crack open. It is not even possible for you to know. The warmth that surrounds the egg and the forces without which it could not incubate, are God in many forms. Sometimes you are aware of what is inside the egg and sometimes you are more aware of what is outside the egg, clumsy as this metaphor may be. When you focus on Teacher both outside and inside the egg, then there is no discrepancy between Soul and personality. Although We separate things out from each other for the purpose of definition and understanding, you must always put them back together in the end. Soul and personality are not, in essence, two different things. Look at yourself as this totality in all things. In that way, you reject nothing.*

God says, "I do not turn away from you. It is you who turns away from me." There is nothing here for you but the light, the way to the light and the illumination of all obstacles to the light. It is total surrender that is required, the total and complete offering of one's being for the sake of transformation.

More deep distress with Izzi. She totaled her car and miraculously, and I mean miraculously, escaped any serious injury. Careening across five lanes of L.A. highway without being hit by a single other car feels like a one in a million occurrence. She said she wasn't drunk, but I don't know. It is no accident that You are talking about complete surrender.

I am heartened to see that the old feelings of self-pity and feeling unloved by God are just not there and have no pull for me. I spoke honestly and directly to her, even though it was difficult. Then I chanted with all my heart and I felt very connected, no complaints, no requests except to be shown the way to more and more surrender.

At that time, I sometimes went to chant at a local Satsang because I wanted to have more contact with other people. But I was not comfortable there. I had been excited to bow at Muktananda's feet back in the ashram days. I believed that the guru was outside me back then. But now I was being directed to the guru within and I didn't want to bow at *anyone's* feet.

I feel so uncomfortable at the Satsang when everyone bows to the Guru at the end. It feels like I am making something external that I want to keep internal. I want to bow to the Guru inside me, not outside me.

*Do you know that the Guru, Teacher, Soul does not care one iota if you bow or not? The power of any form lies in what stands behind it. You are not asked, ever, to live solely in the **form** of any teaching. There are most certainly times when submission to a form is helpful and even perhaps needed, but that is strictly between you and the Teacher within you. Therefore, your instincts not to hand your inner authority over to anyone are perfect at this time. Forcing something on yourself that does not feel right to you is **not** the surrender We speak of. **There is NO forcing in surrender. Surrender is a heart response to the call of soul within you.** Try not bowing at the Satsang if you want to. Try having the experience of Darshan be strictly between you and the Guru within.*

*God's presence has nothing to do with how you bow or don't bow, nothing to do with your accomplishments or good deeds. **It has nothing to do with anything visible at all.***

I think this was (and still is) one of the hardest "truths" to absorb. The conditioning to become "good," to always strive to become "better," is so pervasive that it easily and automatically overshadows the profound truth that God loves us exactly as we are, that God and Soul are always trying to help us access the love that is ALREADY THERE, NOT perfect the form in order to become worthy of it.

I want to ask for more help with Izzi.

Let your feelings rise and fall as they will. Look for the permanence within the impermanence, for the Self within the personality. The Self can actually take action. Stand in the light of all Our Love and emanate that. Stand in the Self, watch the waves of your personality come and go, and speak to yourself from Soul, which is of course exactly what We do. Know that you can do this anytime, anywhere, computer or no computer, pen and paper or no pen and paper.

You see, We are the Rock of the World, that which does not move, that which does not change no matter how big the waves, no matter how hard they pound on your shore or any shore, no matter for how long. We are the Rock of the World. Stand with Us. Breathe with Us.

I want to say that Your presence in my life every day feels like a visitation from God that has changed my life forever. Thank You for persevering with me. Thank you for the great wisdom you give to me so freely. Thank you for being inside me so that I *experience* what You tell me. Thank you for believing in me when I don't believe in myself.

We love you. Notice that sometimes you hear Us knocking on your door and you turn away. Right at that very moment, all you have to do is lift your eyes to see Us and know that We have come to bring you to the light, not to mock you or shame you or judge you or reject you. All you have to do is open your door and We will come in—ALWAYS. It is your own self-judgment that closes the door, not God's lack of love for you or indifference. There is no lack of love or indifference of any kind IN REGARD TO ANYONE in Oneness.

*This is the forgiveness of Christ. Christ does not sit in front of a big book, read off the list of ill deeds committed by each individual, and then wipe the page clean because he is such a nice man or because you have asked in just the right way in just the right church. The forgiveness of Christ is not even something bestowed on you. **It is something You and Christ Consciousness do Together**. Do you understand this? When you (or anyone) stand before the Lord, in whatever state of darkness or ignorance or pain, and you do not turn away but YOU INVITE THE LORD INTO YOUR HOUSE, EXACTLY AS IT IS, WITH A PURE HEART, YOU ARE PARTICIPATING IN THE FORGIVENESS OF CHRIST. You see a completely new word is needed. Christ doesn't really forgive anything. **There is nothing to forgive**. Christ Consciousness is the entrance into what is most holy so that you may transform the House of your Being into a Temple of God. **It is not about making your house perfect: it is about loving the house the Lord has given you.** When you judge yourself unworthy, **you** close the door and **you** have **condemned yourself** to the hell of your own supposed limitations. You see now? God does not do that, Man does.*

Chapter XII

M other Earth opens her doors to me again...

I *got it* as much as any mother of a self-destructive child might get it—that you stay close to your own truth and your own heart's direction in relation to the disease you cannot control—because that is actually all you *can* do, no matter how unbearable the powerlessness is you feel, no matter how great the need to "save," no matter how intense the feelings of personal failure are that you beat yourself up with even though you know better. I *got it*, but the pain was no less. I still feared the black face of death *even if it is cause for celebration* in a far off heaven.

But They were not talking about codependency and enabling, boundaries, limit setting, or self-care, though of course all those concepts were helpful and needed. They were talking massive principles here—not projecting or accepting projections, knowing that there is a soul purpose for all life experiences and relationships, that everything and everyone is Teacher in a multitude of forms. They were talking about seeing ourselves, *exactly* as we are, as temples of God—not in theory but in consciousness, about karma and Return and the Road Home and "maps" for the journey that we can learn to read. The landscape was breathtaking. The particular place where I was on that road was still terrifying.

And even so, Mother Earth opened her arms to me again. If there were proof that God's love is not conditional in any way, this would surely be one more outstanding example.

I went out into the hot tub to focus on my body. I am trying to love myself and undo a lifetime of judgment. I talked with You directly in my head, sitting out there under the stars, and the most astonishing conversation occurred. I heard You tell me to look at the brightest star in the sky and feel Your energy which I did even though a part of me thought this was really hokey. I actually began to feel the energy. There was a flowing conversation with You and the bare outline of it was about working to eliminate the negative energies that are still attached to my body. I was able to be with my naked body in the water, to feel it. I looked down at my breasts and my belly and You told me that my body is exactly the body I am supposed to have, that it is the right shape and form.

You told me I am The Mother of the Earth, exactly those words. And there was so much power behind the words I felt knocked out by them. You said it is not that the Earth is your child, but you are mother *from* the Earth, mother rising out of the Earth. What You said was breathtaking. You whispered to me so gently that so very much is possible if you allow the light in.

*This is the goddess quality of the energy that is truly possible to experience through the female body. The body you have is this Mother from the Earth body **because that IS the female body.** It's not that Phyllis is Mother from the Earth; it is **Woman** that is Mother from the Earth. Honor and love your woman body in this divine aspect. You cannot do that with your present feelings about the body you have. Your female body is the Temple you live in and in which you bow down.*

I almost heard more than one voice just now, one that seemed impatient with me for taking so long to get it.

It is not impatience. It is a poke in your ribs about daring to live in totally uncharted territory. Dare! What if you let yourself feel and breathe and think and move as Mother from the Earth? What if you give that as a divine gift to your body? Do you see that We are helping you clear the body you inhabit in Our unique way? We are sending you energy that is of the purest, highest quality and We are telling you that it is here in unbelievable abundance right now.

Go out into nature this weekend alone. Find your spot and talk with Us. We will be there.

We do not need you to have a skinny body. We need you to have a loved body, a body you allow yourself to enter fully, a body that is your friend and assistant, not one that you perceive as an enemy and a threat and an object of shame. We do not care about style or what modern men find sexually appealing or what you think they find appealing. We care about the seeds still growing in your womb that do not find nourishment because you judge the shape of that womb. Is it not ridiculous? Look at ancient statues and fetishes of mother earth. Look at the bellies. They were honored and adored as sacred. You are not only a woman; you are a pregnant woman, a pregnant mother afraid of her own conception, afraid to give birth. Hold this belly, love this belly, and honor this belly just as you love the thousand-fold births inherent in Mother Earth herself. WE ARE ALL THIS. You see?

The static you feel, the chaos and fight you feel inside when you ovulate or when you menstruate is the charge attached to the tremendous power of the possibility of conception of new life forms that moves inside you. As long as you do not understand this, you misinterpret it as inner conflict that you unconsciously seek to discharge wherever you can. This is a sacred energy, very high in nature, very sacred to be a woman. Very sacred. Never forget this. Bow down to this energy and let it speak to you about Creation. Do you not imagine there was tremendous re-organization of energies when this world was created? That form was not preceded by chaos? In microcosm, this is what every woman is entitled to participate in inside her own body. WE ARE ALL THIS. EACH AND EVERY ONE.

I don't know what to think. My ego is even blown away, nothing for it to hold onto.

Do what you need to do and give your body some rest. We are here. Allow what has happened to move inside you like a gentle stream flowing. Surrender your mind as you have known it to be. Tomorrow is a big day.

...Today I will be going out into nature alone to meet You and meet myself as You said and I found myself subtly fearing it or resisting in the way I sometimes resist writing. And then the whole issue of where can I go, because I don't feel safe going out into nature alone. A friend suggested a place in Tesuque that is very private but near town, where there is a beautiful stream and a little beach. So even though I pictured myself somewhere much more desert-like, I felt I would start there.

On the way, I noticed my mind filled with critical thoughts. The same old stuff– you're so unconscious, look at you. This very special thing is about to happen and you don't prepare yourself, you are totally unconscious, blah, blah, blah. But somehow, You were right there in the car with me. I don't remember now anything You said, but somehow Your presence reconnected me and I felt so foolish that I make myself miserable with my relentlessly critical mind.

The Earth has something to say to you today. That is the purpose for this trip.

So I drove to Tesuque and found the stream and immediately I felt I was in the wrong place. I did not feel connected to that spot at all and I wanted to leave and find a place that looked more like my Arizona desert. But I heard You tell me not to go yet, that I needed to be by the water for a while. So I put my things down while my head was still full of non-acceptance of being there and yet I was there.

I took out my notebook to write about the hard time I was giving myself when I heard You tell me very clearly to go stand in the water. I had thought I should take off my plastic flip-flops before I left and put on tennis shoes because I didn't know where I would be walking, but for some reason I decided not to. So here I was with the perfect thing on my feet to walk into the water with and I did. It was very cold, but I stood there until I felt I should go back and write. This is what You said.

We have no need for you to be in a certain state or frame of mind at all times. Don't you see, if you were supposed to be other than you are, you would be? Yesterday We told you to go do what you needed and wanted to do. We didn't say you must meditate all day or chant. Your son said, "Wow Mom, you must be in an incredibly receptive state" when you told him We said to go out into nature and that We would speak to you there. You are, and it is nothing compared to what will come. Do your daily life. Do it with love, acceptance, and as much happiness as you can. We will let you know exactly what We want you to do. We have been doing that all along. Give yourself a break! There is no judgment of you in Us.

We told you that this day is about receiving messages from the Earth. That is why you have to come to water first. Go back and stand in the water. (Which I did.)

You see, Darling, We try so hard to tell you that there is nothing to do wrong. This moment is as it should be. You will be perfectly here until you are perfectly done being here and then you will perfectly move to the next aspect of your journey. That is the essence of universal perfection. And all the time, of course, you will go nowhere but UP, TO US, HOME, TO GOD. You see, Darling? This is only a level of reality through which you will move in your ascent. Your particular task is to translate certain aspects of this level into English, you might say. What you fear is not Us or anything higher than your known world. All you fear is your own self-judgment. You see how happy you are here? Why make it so hard for yourself to come? Go stand in the water.

I stand in the water. The Earth says to me,

I am crying as you have cried. Water brings this message to you. I am crying as you have cried. You see, just as you are Soul and the bird is Soul, and the bush and the sky and the light on the water– all are Soul– so I, the Earth, also am Soul. I cry for the return of spirit. I cry for the wrongs done to my body as you have cried for the wrongs done to yours. And just like you, my tears and my pain are wrapped around my Soul and are the entry point to Soul just as your pain was the door for you. We are travelling the same road.

I miss you, Mother, where have you been so long? We were not meant to be separate, you and I. You knew this but you did not understand. You did not know the way to me though I called out to you and you called out to me. I ask you to stand in my flowing water as one invited into the veins of my heart's blood, flowing from the very center of me. You stand in the water to feel and hear my heart beat and read it and write it. I am lonely for my sisters and my brothers. We were never meant to travel this whole way alone. You were never meant to be without me nor I you.

You see, ALL IS SACRED. The water is sacred, the dirt, the rocks, the plants– all is sacred, holy, a temple unto itself. The Earth, I, am one of the most beautiful temples of God ever manifested. You are to see and feel each atom as a sacred manifestation of the Creator. Live in this.

You are struggling with being called Mother of the Earth, Mother from the Earth. You would rather be called little sister. Mother implies too much maturity, too much power for you. But you cannot give yourself another name. Stand in the water and feel your body, your breasts and your hips and your legs and arms as Mother and sacred and connected to Earth's life's blood. Let it flow into you and through your veins. Make this connection.

Message from the Water:

I have carried so many so far. I ask you to carry me one step here along this Way. I am the life-blood of the Earth. Feel me enter your own veins and flow into your life-blood. We are One, Mother. Carry me with words now. My language used to be understood freely but no longer.

This is your Baptism. Do you understand now why baptism is about Water? You, of course, know nothing about Christian Baptism. But We tell you now that when you are immersed in Water, OUR RIVERS FLOW AS ONE. That is the Baptism of Christ. Your consciousness becomes one with Our consciousness. Human consciousness merges with Earth Consciousness. That is the level and the scale on which Christ participated in the Divine. You also know nothing about the meaning of The Father, The Son, and the Holy Ghost. We tell you the meaning now. The Father is God, the Creator. The Son is You, the individual created. It is also the bird, the rock at your foot and the mountain behind you. The Holy Ghost is all the rest of Creation in relation to the Son and the Father. The Father is the Infinite reaching out a hand to the Son, the Finite, and the Holy Ghost is all the rest of Creation in which the Father and Son together participate. That is the Three in the One, for all is God, all, beginning to end. Baptism is an initiation into this Holy Trinity.

You see, We all Return TOGETHER. That is why We cry out to you today to hear Our call. WE ALL RETURN TOGETHER.

Thank you. Thank You.

***

Yesterday seems like a monumental day and yet I still feel like a very ordinary person. You told me that I don't need to be anything other than ordinary, that if I were supposed to be some larger than life figure experiencing all this, then I would be. I think I really have a belief that I should be living in an elevated state all the time or else I am doing something wrong or I am not doing enough. I am shocked by the contrast between my ordinariness and these incredible experiences that are taking me farther and farther from the known world I have lived in up until now. I am unconsciously assuming that because there is this contrast, I must be deficient in some way. I heard You say that I don't have to sprout wings in order to be worthy.

You see you have so many misconceptions. In your culture the ego rules. The bigger the ego, often the greater the "success" of an individual. You are very conditioned by this. Everyone is. You have no framework for success that does not boost ego. Your poor little ego just doesn't know what to do here **because "success" in Our World is related to the SHEDDING of ego structures and ego patterns of thought and feeling.**

We know that you are very uncomfortable that so much of this process focuses on you. You fear being judged by others as self-serving. Why do you persist in making this judgment when even you know it isn't true? You have not learned how to receive without the gift being a token of your worth. This is what it means to be caught in ego. Do you see this? When you give a gift to your child, you do so because the love in your heart finds expression in that moment in the gift you have given, whether it is a kiss on the cheek or $1000. You do not give the gift because the child has earned your love, is worthy of your love. You may be proud of your child and what he or she has done, **but your love and your gifts are based on your ability to experience love in your own heart and on your ability and desire to give that love.** *Who is more able to experience Love in the Heart of Self than God? That is how you are loved. That is how ALL are loved. That is the place from which these gifts are given. That is the place in yourself from which you must learn to receive. This is the difference between conditional* *love and unconditional love. You are still living in a world of conditional love in relation to Phyllis Leavitt. Therefore, you think you have to keep proving your worth as God pours Love over you. If God were judging you by the same standards you judge yourself, there would be no words on this page.*

You cringe at the focus being on you? Would you rather We recite dry theory to you? **There is no Teaching apart from you. The Teacher exists IN RELATION to the disciple.** *Every atom of your being, every light beam of your Soul, of every Soul, is going* **Home**. *Do you think a theory apart from the personal will do that trick? Do you think it would even matter if you had the most exact formulation in the world?*

This is what your Baptism is about. When you are washed in the Earth's life's blood, your ego is washed away. The ego has no power in the river in which you stood. Your poor little injured ego, which has believed for centuries and centuries that it was bad, is still trying to make itself good. Give it up and get into the river. It calls to you. How can you possibly hold truly sacred the rock, the tree, and the water in the stream if you do not hold yourself sacred with every breath? Do you understand now why the focus is on you? There will come a day when there will no longer be a "you" as you know yourself now. You see, when you truly hold yourself sacred, you will cease to be as you have known yourself to be.

We translate what you need to hear. After that, it is washed away like a picture in the sand. In the end, you will not need any of these words.

***

My only association with Baptism was that it was a ritual immersion in water symbolic of pronouncing the one submerged a "Christian." It was not lost on me that my "Baptism" had nothing to do with anything "Christian" whatsoever, that it had nothing to do with conversion or religion. My Baptism was an initiation into a level of Earth Consciousness, into the awareness that we are all one life, all one organism. The call of my Earth Mother and the Voice of this God that spoke to me of soul and the Road Home suddenly came together. Their circles intersected and I was allowed to stand where they met.

It did not seem to matter at all to Mother Earth and God that I was not the most powerful *human* mother, that my baby was flirting with death and I didn't know what to do. You took me anyway and Baptized me in the Water of Your life. You Baptized me, the wandering Jew out alone in the desert of a Twentieth century life.

***

AND, when the pure magic of the experience settled, it was also not lost on me that Your use of terminology from the Christian Bible – Baptism, the Father, the Son and the Holy Ghost– in a context *completely outside* any little bit of Christianity I was familiar with-- felt like a set-up for *heresy*. Once again, there was a feeling of, "Oh my God, why are You using *these* words?

Chapter XIII

T asked me if I could try getting a message from Them for a man he knew. I was very hesitant to do it– very. I did not see myself as a psychic and did not want that role. However, despite myself I immediately heard something about this man and so I just did the reading then and there. I seemed to get very specific information about what life struggles he was facing and apparently, what I said was very accurate and helpful. Later, T asked me to do readings for other people. I was always frightened and very resistant to the request but I felt I should try to overcome my fears. Before each one, I would say a prayer that was very simple. *I am not afraid. I will get out of the way. I trust.*

One day, completely unsolicited by either T or myself, I received a message for T while I was writing and it totally freaked me out. I just felt like NO, I'm not doing this. I felt I was stepping way out of bounds in our relationship. I felt sure I would only be seen as presumptuous to have a message for the person who was helping me. I left my house utterly distraught, like I'm going to walk away from all this right now. I wanted to throw in the towel.

Eventually, I came back and wrote. By that time, I was sure my reaction of fear and denial was a further sign that I was not worthy of all They had given me. I just couldn't get away from self-judgment. This is what They said:

We are not come to hurt you in any way. You do know that. The One who walks with you is indeed a very loving and wise master and there is no such thing as disappointment in you. Are you disappointed when a baby stumbles trying to walk? No, of course not. You are happy to see the baby try so hard to stand on her own. If she falls, you encourage her to get up and try again, because you know that every time she gets up, she builds her self-confidence and strengthens exactly those leg muscles needed for walking. At the same time, you don't pick the baby up every time she falls either, because you want her to learn to walk and the baby wants to learn to walk. No matter how much you love the baby, you cannot actually walk for her. That is how We are in relation to you. We are your biggest cheering section.

*You are asked to focus on the Teacher within. All these people can live their lives without a reading from you, but you cannot live the life you came here to live without offering your total being to your Soul and obeying every word. Your practice of surrendering into a **pure heart** space is exactly what you are to do. What **you experience** in listening for a message for someone is all that matters. That is what it means to focus on the Teacher within rather than on the message. The message is for **you. How much food another picks up from your plate is their decision and a part of their path. Your path is to put out on your plate the food you have to give. But your focus should be on what you have to LEARN, not on what you have to GIVE.** Remember, every time you hesitate to trust, you clog the channel. And that is okay. Just notice it and the more you can catch it, the easier it will be to trust the next time.*

Part of what you are working on right now is clearing the channel within yourself. Nothing is to stick to this channel, nothing. Look at it as a throat. You eat. If your food continually stuck to the sides of your throat, soon your throat would be blocked. You would not be able to eat anymore and you would starve. Psychically this is how people die.

They are clogged with their own selves. Their issues, unfinished business, and all the projected energies they have allowed in and projected out are stuck to the sides of their throats, undigested, until they expire. To make use of this clumsy metaphor, you are to take only what you need from the food you eat, digest it, and expel all the rest. Psychically, that is what you are working on. Say your prayer every morning—I am not afraid, I will step out of the way, I trust.

The great fear you carry has to do with former lifetimes of persecution. You were burned at the stake as a witch. You were called crazy for what you knew and what you said and the psychic memory of that has made you extremely susceptible to the word "crazy" now. The bind you experience is that as you come into full contact with the inner wisdom you are blessed with, the fear of being persecuted, burned at the stake, is so great that you immediately make the first association that comes to you and that is that you are crazy. However, in the lifetime We speak of, being labeled crazy did not save you either, though there were those that tried valiantly to hide you behind that shield. The church was after you and they burned you anyway, crazy or not, as a heretic. Your unconscious tendency now is to retreat into feeling crazy when you feel threatened by the power of what you know.

You don't have to walk that road anymore, not in this lifetime.

And so, yet another door opened, totally unexpected– the door into past lives.

I get so afraid that I make all this up. So it was a leap of faith that I let myself hear You tell me about my past life and yet, despite all the doubt that came up, it all feels true. It explains feelings I could not explain from this lifetime alone. You told me that the door is now open for me to look at as many past lives as I want to, however many I need to better understand my patterns and my purpose. I have decided that no matter how much doubt tries to overtake me, I am going to open that door. It may be very difficult for me and at the same time, judging by the information I already got, I think it will be invaluable. The dynamic inside me that You explained was something no one ever would have been able to identify or explain for me, and I don't believe I could have done it for myself.

When you open the door to your own past lives, you will have no further doubt that it can be done for others and that it can be helpful for others, just as you now know by your own experience that it is possible to come out of the long dark tunnel of childhood abuse and pain. You want to know more about the witch lifetime.

I'm going out again. Can all this really be true?

Okay, time out. These are the rules: NO EDITING. NONE. Otherwise, you distort the full message. Do you understand why We stopped you here? You cannot edit what is told to you. It is not just that it will affect the message but also you must understand that your mind as it is does not have this information. It is being given to you. The process by which the information is given to you is sometimes dramatic, sometimes extraordinarily subtle. Try not to comment on what you hear. Simply write it down exactly as it is given. The information builds on itself in the translating from Us to you.

So yes, Izzi was your daughter in that lifetime also. The little girl you saw in a vision when you were pregnant with Izzi was her. Do you remember being struck, after she was born, by the fact that the vision showed a little girl with light brown curly hair and that is not what Izzi looks like? That is because you saw her form as it was in that previous incarnation. Do you remember that there was an intense emotion that welled up along with the visual image? That emotion was one of recognition spanning lifetimes.

You were burned as a witch by the church. In that lifetime, you had a very deep love of Christ. You were one who experienced his presence, both in your heart and visually. You have had the grace to see visions in many lifetimes. That lifetime was particularly powerful. You tried to share your love of Christ with those around you. You believed that your direct experience of Christ would be seen as pleasing to those in the church. However, your naiveté and innocence were threatening and the more personal your experience became, the more you were at risk. You never fully understood what you had "done wrong." In the end, some of those who loved you tried to shield you by describing your experience as "crazy." You suffered greatly in this because, while this defense might have held the possibility of reprieve, it also signified the betrayal of your beliefs and your faith. In the end, this dilemma did much to drive you "crazy." You died believing you had betrayed your lord. Emotionally and spiritually, this devastating lifetime has remained with you as a blueprint in the life you now live.

However, what you did not understand then is that the trials of that life, terrible as they were, were exactly what you incarnated to experience– not the fire per se, but the challenge of faith and its expression in the world. The struggle to stay true to your beliefs is a hallmark of many lifetimes. As you see, it is a hallmark of this one as well.

*Fire is a symbol of your path. Fire is always a transformative event. Fire does not occur without transforming physically all it encounters. In the very same way, fire also transforms emotional, mental, and spiritual energy. The transformative effect of this particular fire on your path is only now emerging. Your psyche went into a profound state of shock in that death which was carried over into this lifetime, the shock of one who is essentially naive and innocent. All of this has been a part of your path. Nothing was a mistake. Nothing was overlooked. All was as it was intended **by your own Soul** to be. You are working now with many of the same themes.*

*You see, just as We told you not to edit one word of what is said because there is a building process to the unfolding of this information, **so too, there is a building process in moving from one body to another**. One lifetime builds upon all the previous incarnations to a perfect culmination, so to speak, of creation of experience. Not to be elucidated now. You wanted to know why you left* *that life in a state of psychic shock. And We say now only that that is what was required as a building block for this life.*

We will tell you this much. When you leave a life in that kind of shock, the veil between the worlds remains thinned. The shock prevents completion and the lack of completion prevents psychic closure, so that a wider door than usual remains open between one life and the next. This is a chosen and intended experience and not necessarily the only way it can happen.

Izzi was your daughter and when you died, she was about three. The vision you had of her during your pregnancy was your last sight of her in that lifetime, looking back at you, not understanding what was happening but connected to you deeply. In this lifetime, among many other themes that will unfold, Izzi has the same deep connection to you, but the pain of losing you in that lifetime was so great for her that she came this time determined to separate from you before you could ever be separated from her. Bill was a man of the church. While he was not the one directly responsible for your death, he stood by and did not try to prevent it. He also had a great love for you in that lifetime. Love may not be the exact word but it was more like awe mixed with personal feelings of affection for you and for your direct connection to Christ. That awe became envy and that is why he did nothing to help you. He watched you die knowing you did not deserve to, but to acknowledge that would have meant he would have had to admit that his own faith was a pretense, that he wished to feel spirit but did not yet feel it. Therefore, he remained silent and stony and the more he saw your anguish, the stonier and more resentful he became of you.

Eddie (my older son) *was your husband. He did not share your experience nor did he refute it. He respected you to the end. He tried to help by professing your insanity though he knew it was not true and he later regretted that. In this lifetime, he is extremely sensitive to your pain but he has difficulty taking it in and appears often to not want to know about it or hear about it because of his former helplessness.*

However, he very much wants to take care of you in some way this time around and to stand in his own integrity of the truth. Daniel (my younger son) *was not with you in that life. However, in spirit form, he was waiting to be born to you and did not have the opportunity. Your mother is the one that had you killed. Your father is a stuck entity over many incarnations and We will look at that later when you are ready.*

You would think I might have balked at all this and walked away right then and there. Wasn't it bad enough that I was already the black sheep in my present day family, the one who just couldn't "find herself," the one who let the nice Jewish doctor go, was too introspective, too mixed up in crazy spiritual groups? Wasn't it bad enough that I had already caused my parents so much pain with my insistence on memories from *this life* that no one really believed anyway? And now I'm saying that a Divine voice is telling me that my parents were instrumental in my death in a past life? Really, what next? I ask my parents to do therapy with me around our past life relationships?

But you see, I did not feel *any* of that *or* walk away, not at all, because every word rang absolutely true, like puzzle pieces that just snap into place and you finally begin to see the bigger picture. Yet again, I was presented with an irrefutable internal reality that both heightened my fear of exposure, of condemnation, of heresy, AND brought me another step closer to Home in myself. Could we, would we, one day devise a therapy that accounts for the evolution of soul through various incarnations?

Let me add here that I no longer feel blame for my mother and father. And, I am also sure that the way my family perceived our various parts is not the same as the way I experienced them. In the big picture, I know now that it is not about who is right and who is wrong. We all do the best we can with the paths we chose and were chosen for, and the parts themselves are less important that the learning and the evolution of consciousness available through them. If we truly chose each other for the sake of the evolution of souls, then there is nothing to either blame or forgive, but only to honor, accept, and walk through, however and wherever our own souls direct us. And from that place there is only love for my parents.

I understand that now, and I have a sense of what it feels like to see everyone who walks with me (which is actually everyone on earth) in that way, but back then I had to walk through many fires before this understanding could even begin to become real. And so I just went where They took me.

I am in awe that You take me so far so fast. Sitting out on the back porch this morning, I looked up at the moon in the morning sky and felt the air and the earth around me and I saw lifetimes as a Native American and understood even more deeply my connection to the desert. I feel I have the possibility of getting a vast overview of my entire incarnation process. Yesterday, after You talked to me about not editing for any purpose, the writing came so fast I could hardly keep up with it. It felt like a dam broke and a flood began to pour through. The only place where I could not let anything flow was when it came to my father. I have felt a lot of tenderness for my father in this life, a need for his love, and a desire to protect him. It hurt me to see that I was unable to follow Your rules there and You so kindly came forward and let me know that the connection to my father has been extremely problematic over several lifetimes and that it is okay that I am not yet ready to deal with it. It was a great relief. I did not want to see more and You helped me accept that.

I saw that one of the issues I carry from the witch life is that I felt tortured by the pain caused to my family. And that accounts for the feelings I carry now of being almost immobilized by the thought that my truth, *this writing*, will be unbearable for those who love me.

I did some work with the witch lifetime in a session with T. I saw that the one who was Bill in that life has an enormous amount of compassion waiting for him and all around him, just as was explained to me earlier that God surrounds and waits for everyone and everything to Return. I saw, too, that the one who killed her and the ones who stood behind him, had huge issues of hatred and lust and envy with women and they killed those women not for their religious beliefs, not really. They tortured and killed them for some kind of twisted pleasure derived from inflicting great humiliation and physical degradation as well as great physical pain on women. I saw that it *looked* like fanatical religious zeal, but for many of these men, it was somehow sexually gratifying and empowering to dominate and destroy the Body of Woman.

This you can now know. The infliction of pain and degradation is always the case in war of any kind, whether it is war between nations or war on an ethnic group or war on women, blacks, Jews, gays, or other minorities. Hear this message. Willful acts of violence against the sacredness of any incarnated form stem from a force many call Satan or the Devil or Sin or Evil, but these names give a wrong impression. We call it The Shadow of the Holy Ghost. This force of destruction is the shadow side of the Duality of Light and Darkness.
*No one ever starts a war for the value called freedom or the value called socialism or communism, not in Reality. War, the assault of one human being on another, is waged from a place of disconnection from soul, disconnection from the value of life itself AND it is waged from the ego-based belief that people are entitled to impose their values and ideologies **through violence**. (We are not referring here to aggression*

that is clearly an act of self-defense, though in the realm of ego, the issue of justifiable self-defense could likely be debated from here to eternity.)

War, killing and destruction, are not CAUSED by differing beliefs. The differing beliefs only provide the arena that appears to justify aggression. *This truth is one that your entire world has been struggling to work through to consciousness for a long, long time.* **Strength, conviction, and power have been separated from wisdom, tolerance, patience, and love. The Masculine energies of action and assertion have lost their connection to the Feminine energies of nurturance and receptivity.** *The result is the "arming" of the extremes of what is considered masculine that cannot tolerate the receptive, connected nature of the feminine* **within themselves**. *This* **dis-owning of the feminine** *allows for massive projection of weakness, inferiority, shame and blame onto others. This is also why in war and in any arena where excessive physical force becomes the modus operandi, you see such overt violence perpetrated on women and on anyone perceived as less-than in any way.*

***

Over and over again, I had the experience of diving deep into the painful themes of my personal existence only to find that the door immediately opened to the overriding *principles of operation* of ego consciousness as they manifest in human functioning and behavior on the Horizontal Plane. Over time, I was shown in greater and greater detail how the personal themes we each individually carry and play out over lifetimes are microcosmic snapshots of world themes being enacted by the entire human race and that these themes are all related to specific energies of Creation taking finite form. Much of this information doesn't appear until later in the writing. What I was being shown at that time was that we each, down to the smallest details of our personal lives, play a knowable part in the evolution of human consciousness — the great descent into darkness and the emergence into light, the birth of ego and the rebirth of soul. We both crystalize out into our individual parts and we all Return together.

And we can participate in that Return with consciousness.

The energies at play in your witch lifetime were a microcosm of many of the most unconscious and destructive energies that are struggling to Push Through to consciousness in the world today. **The SEPARATION of Masculine and Feminine opens the door to the assaultive, murderous impulses of the Shadow of the Holy Ghost and together they act upon the human race as a psychic virus, deadlier than AIDS, because what is afflicted here are the pipelines to Soul. The pipelines to Soul become so clogged that the voice of Soul is as THE VOICE OF ONE CRYING IN THE WILDERNESS.**

This is why Earth spoke to you. There is a cry going out **to the human race to come Home.** *There is a cry going out to see the magnitude of the forces that are being played out here. When you— either as a single human being or as a race of beings— lose sight of the sacredness of the necessary interconnection of Masculine and Feminine energies, lose sight of the sacredness of the sexes, male and female, lose sight of the sacredness of the sexual act as a mirror in microcosm of the Act of Creation of the Worlds, and thus lose sight of the sacredness of all life on Earth, you open the door to war and disease and greed and despair, and the list goes on and on.*

In the witch lifetime and in your world today, aggression has become sexualized, sex has become an instrument of aggression, sometimes very overtly and sometimes more hidden in what some people like to call healthy experimentation.

***

I was out in the hot tub last night and as I looked at the stars and the sky it brought back so many times when I was young that I would try to conceive of infinity. How could the universe have no end, no edge where it stops? But then, what would be on the other side of that edge if there were one? You said—

*There cannot possibly be an end to the universe because the universe is a manifestation of God and God is Infinite. Just as God has Infinite Mercy, Love, Compassion, Wisdom, and Power, God also has **Infinite Form**. You, in your finite state of mind, can only **imagine** infinity, think of it conceptually. It is not a concept. Infinity is a Reality.*

Chapter XIV

And so, what was opened up in my personal Baptism, which took place not in the River Jordan with angels and saints but right here in a more or less backyard stream in Tesuque, New Mexico in 1995– what was opened up was a doorway to the sacredness of our interconnection with all life here on earth and the understanding that the Road of Return is about all of us returning together, all of us meaning the living organism of the Earth and all her kingdoms, not just the human kingdom. My personal journey was only one small fragment of EARTH'S JOURNEY. And it just rippled out from there. Mother earth had more to say.

I went out on the porch in the morning and sat in my back yard. Two golden orioles were fluttering around in a tree not far from me. I have never seen them before and the beauty of their golden bellies and faces is awe-inspiring. I had the thought to ask the oriole if he had something to say to me, and even though I thought it was somewhat stupid, I felt fear at asking. But immediately I heard, "Yes, I am very beautiful. I am pure gold. People love to look at me and the gold of my feathers is just like the gold that comes out of the earth. But this is the real reason I am so beautiful: number one, because I was created in the image of God, and number two, so that all who look at me will be reminded of the Creator and the beauty of the Creator. That is my function. So many have lost sight of that and when they see beauty, they want to *have* it. How can you have God? God has you. I am only one small reminder that God is everywhere."

Then I saw a tiny unremarkable looking little brown bird sitting on a telephone wire and wanted to ask the same thing and again came the fear and again I pushed through it and he said, "Don't be ridiculous! You think because I am drab to your way of thinking I could not have a beautiful message like the oriole? You think to yourself, well, every little bird around can't have a message. You also thought for a moment that only the beautiful and those that stand out would have a message. That is not true. This is my message to you: I am a manifestation of the living power of God. I, this little bird sitting on a wire, looking this way and that, appearing to be doing nothing useful or out of the ordinary, am a conduit of Creation. I bring form to spirit as does every atom, every creature, every element, and every movement in this universe. I bring form to spirit as you do, as every living person does. This is anything but drab. This is as holy as can be. **When you allow the Earth to speak to you, there is nothing but God everywhere.** Please hear this: THIS IS NOT JUST AN IDEA OR A SPIRITUAL DOCTRINE. THIS IS A LIVING TRUTH. When you ask to talk to me, to the oriole, or to the water or the rock, you are asking ENTRY into the world of the LIVING TRUTH OF GOD. Therefore, it is not unreasonable to have fear, but now you can know that fear by its proper name. It is AWE. It is REVERENCE. Never ask lightly.

When you were asked to stand in the Water, you were being initiated into THIS. That was your initiation into a new level of Consciousness. You have actually been here before, many times. We welcome you back, Mother. Welcome, with all our hearts."

Again and again, the love that was so generously given to me from so many directions broke through the tight container of my still frightened little personality. It seemed to find me everywhere. I suppose it was only natural that such an inpouring of love left me even lonelier in the human world.

For whatever reason, good or bad, I still feel lonely even with all that is miraculous in my life now, still long to be in a relationship.

We will tell you this: You are not in a relationship with a man right now because he is not here yet. It is as simple as that. You heard Us say that he is coming but you do not want to write that down because you are afraid to have hope. He is not here yet. No other reason. Not because you are unlovable or ugly or boring or not sexy or old– none of the above. And part of the reason he is not here yet you already know, and that is because We, your soul, want you to do this work very intensively right now. You do not want to believe what We say. You rather wish We had said that you really are meant to be alone for the rest of your life, that We are asking you to be a monk. We are not asking that. You do not want to have hope because it hurts too much, because the pain in relationship has been so very great. Know that all is perfect at every moment. That if you long for something and it does not come, that you are meeting yourself here exactly as you need to do. This is a time to open your heart to the power of absolute and total surrender.

You can go on wanting whatever it is you want. You must allow that. You have never fully dared to ask to be loved, in the flesh, in this life, in this form, because up until now you have not believed you were lovable. You feel it is foolish to waste Our time asking that a man come to be with you. We tell you not to be ridiculous. We tell you that you have withheld from yourself for so long, that you believe anything given to you is an incredible favor of the universe. That is simply not so.

The message was repeated over and over and yet it was still so difficult to grasp. Our mission here is not to *become* worthy: our mission is to remember that we *already are*. We can ask for everything we want and *learn* from asking, *learn* from receiving or not receiving, and *learn* from wherever that road takes us.

What did the little brown bird say? He said that Divine Love is everywhere, pulsating around you and all humankind, but you do not see it, you do not know it. Now you are beginning to see. Now you are beginning to know. We are telling you to give to yourself even more freely as an act of faith. Tell Us what there is about you that has caused Us to ever withhold anything from you. Our love for you has been and always will be Infinite, Endless, Boundless, and Divine.

*We are here to tell you, to let it be known, that **God's love is truly unconditional**. Man puts conditions in God's mouth– you must do this or that, belong to this religion or do only that practice. Sit down now with your beautiful heart just as it is and ask for exactly what you want and know that what you want is also divine. We told you about sex and aggression and the tremendous opening that combination provides for the Shadow of the Holy Ghost. **Do you not imagine that Love, in which the Masculine and Feminine energies are in balance within two people who honor their purpose with one another, love between any two people who open their hearts to God and Soul—do you not imagine that That Love is not as powerfully healing and life-redeeming to the planet as the other forces are destructive?** We are talking about massive forces here. You have already asked to be a part of that healing for others, for your children and for your clients. You already have the Grace of God. Now you can ask for the Grace of Man.*

Chapter XV

I know something unbelievable has happened. It is endless what I have learned and been allowed to enter into. At the same time, I have suddenly become very sober about it all.

I want with all my heart to say I will never leave You. And even so, if I am really honest, there is still a part of me that wants to run away, wants to just have a normal happy little life and forget I ever knew any of this, wants to go back to some imagined sense of security I never had to begin with. At the same time, I don't want to ever consider *not* being on this path. I don't want to ever feel crazy again, but I see that fear and doubt are not over.

It came up more and more that I would one day share this writing with others on a scale much larger than talking to T about it, doing a few readings, and sharing the writing with some of the other people he was working with. It seemed that if I was to have my voice after all these lifetimes, there would come a time and place where I would speak. I also felt that what was being given to me so lovingly from another realm was not intended to be used solely for my own evolution. Although these intimations felt unquestionably true, they struck terror in me. I could not imagine what it would take for me to have that kind of voice in the world. Maybe in the distant future I would write a book.

I want to tell You honestly from my heart that I don't know if I am ready. I'm not unwilling but I don't know if I'm ready. These are the reasons why. I don't feel I have done enough work of my own. Perhaps I need more direction from You. I have absolutely no desire to be a psychic. My only true desire is to hear the voice of Teacher and follow it. But as I am now, I don't think I'm ready for anything beyond what I am already doing.

Well, how are you going to learn, how are you going to become ready without practice?

That isn't what I wanted to hear, but I'm listening.

Just as you had to start somewhere having sessions as a therapist, and you learned how to be a better therapist with a lot of practice and supervision, you could say that this work will emerge and grow in a similar way. It's okay to see yourself as someone in training, not a perfected master. Why do you think We came to you as powerfully as We do? We want you to know without a doubt that the value of what comes to you comes through the Grace of God, not your hard work. This is not about you working hard. It is about moving beyond fear, getting out of the way, and trusting.

Why did you choose me? Aren't there many better-equipped people out there?

This is a mutual choice. You chose Us exactly the same way We chose you. We are both, so to speak, agreeing to swim with the tide rather than against it. That is the real reason you don't run away. You cannot. You chose this.

I have to admit I have this feeling that I could read a person's face and see their past lives in their face. This could be totally off the wall, but this is what has come to me. My sense is that the whole story is imprinted in the body, that the present body, face, and expressions contain the total psychic, spiritual history of the person, and that it can be read if you know how to look at the person in the right way. I can't say that I "know" how to do it, but I let myself just go there for a few moments with a client this week. I don't know if what I got was just imagination or not, but I saw something that I was able to integrate into our session and it proved to be very meaningful to my client. I almost feel I could do past life readings for others if I wanted to, though I am not sure I want to.

It was impossible for me to accept all this and just be happy. I imagine someone else might have been excited and embraced this experience with open arms. But the visceral fear of exposure burned through me right along side the Love. It was a totally unnerving experience, to say the least, to be hearing the most Divinely loving and wise voice of Soul alone in my room in 1995, at the same time literally fearing a crowd of angry people coming after me screaming, "Heretic!"

So I want to ask You if there is more that You want me to get out of the past life that has come up so strongly? It feels to me that I had many lives in which I was brutally silenced. The issue feels so dense it is difficult to see the present distinct from the past. There is great fear in my body. It's almost as if I forgot that it was fear and I turned it into self-hate in order to protect myself better.

The pattern of assault has run through many lifetimes, often associated with persecution for religious beliefs or other beliefs that are at odds with or threatening to the prevailing culture. You hear Us say that there is a very big picture behind this scenario and that is correct. Do you want to see the big picture?

Yes, I do.

*This is the big picture: There are only so many themes that the human race and the entire planet Earth are working with. The issue that the oriole touched on is one of them– the desire to **have** God's creations rather than share in them, enjoy them and honor them. Increasingly, humans believe they have to dominate and possess. This is both caused by and leads to greater and greater separation of Masculine and Feminine **energies,** greater and greater separation of active assertive energies from receptive, nurturing energies. We are not talking here only about the relationship between men and women, although the attitudes and beliefs men and women have about each other and the behaviors that result from them are certainly critical at this time in history when human beings have such great power to affect their own viability as well as the viability of so many other life forms.*

*Sex is one of the highest and most potent centers of energy available to mankind because it brings together in physical form two fundamental energies of creation. It is a condition of human incarnation that these two energies are split into male and female bodies and masculine and feminine psyches. This is **lawful** and it is one huge element of what **creates ego consciousness**. Over time, the Masculine/Feminine Duality has become so extreme that the Masculine has lost sight of the **need for balance, cooperation, and union** with the Feminine.*

*Very roughly expressed (in general), the female is born with less male light and the male is born with less female light. The masculine is always seeking the feminine and the feminine is always seeking the masculine. On the Horizontal Plane, one does not feel complete without the other. **BUT, at the very same time, the Law of Duality keeps them at odds.** On the Vertical Plane, Masculine and Feminine **energies** reunite as an egg unites with a sperm.*

*Physically the male/female union creates new physical form; **spiritually the union of Masculine and Feminine energies is a key to the birth of soul consciousness**. We are using these words in the broadest, deepest possible sense. Assertive, active Masculine energy is only **one part** of the energy that constructed the world. Receptive,* *nurturing, inclusive Feminine energy is the other aspect. The sperm is nothing without the egg, just as the egg alone cannot create new life. The theme We speak of is the **re-union of Masculine and Feminine energies in consciousness.** This means the two energies, **within any given individual**, come into greater and greater balance, the assertive active energies **in cooperation with** the receptive nurturing energies and vice versa. We are not talking solely about the relationship between men and women, though as We said, it is a critical issue today. We are talking about ALL human relationships—men and women, women and women, men and men. AND, We are talking about the relationships between groups of individuals, and the relationships between individuals and groups with all the other life forms and kingdoms on earth. We are talking about the masculine and feminine energies embodied and expressed in **ALL** relationships—marriage, partnership, parenting, business, political, educational, religious, economic, environmental, global—ALL relationships.*

The re-union of the Masculine and Feminine is what the human race is confronting as its next evolutionary challenge. *What does this mean?*

*In ego consciousness there will always be a struggle or a tension between these apparent opposites, Masculine and Feminine, **which takes the form of Domination and Submission.** The greater the split of these energies, the more you see power being "sexualized" in human behavior because the combination of sex and aggression is experienced as the most powerful combination of forces available to the small self or the ego. Why do you think war and devastation of one race or one country by another is most often characterized by massive rape and sexual torture? What do you think the atomic bomb is but an unbelievably powerful and symbolic orgasm?*

*This impulse of **one person, entity, or group seeking to dominate and subdue another**– this play of Duality informs **all** ego functioning, not just the relationship between men and women. It informs how societies are organized, how laws are developed and enacted, how resources* *are produced and distributed, how religious, political, and social values are formulated, conveyed, and manifested. **The name of the game in ego consciousness is domination/submission,** however subtly or even unrecognizably that game is played. The greater the split between masculine and feminine energies in all these arenas, the greater the sexualization of aggression becomes. The greater the sexualization of aggression becomes, the greater the split... in a continuously intensifying cycle that can only lead to further destruction.*

*On the Road of Return, the two again become one. Masculine and Feminine reunite—**within the psyche** as a state of being, and manifesting as **cooperation with and honoring of the sanctity of all life forms.** On the Road of Return, there is growing understanding that the birth of soul consciousness is possible **only** through the union of these two energies—because there is NO Duality in Soul. Everything that has been split apart to create ego consciousness and ego experience on the Horizontal Plane for humans comes back together in soul.*

*You can find evidence of this growing awareness in people everywhere who are waking up out of the Sleep of Forgetting—in the intensified focus on women's and children's rights globally, in all efforts to honor and accept gay relationships, efforts to help the oppressed, the emphasis on mediation, couples therapy and family therapy, and in efforts to save endangered species and protect natural resources, air, water, and soil. You also find evidence of this growing awareness in organizations of people large and small that are even attempting to embody group governance and ideals of **equality**, cooperation for mutual benefit, elimination of racial, economic, religious and political oppression. Within these people, you see a growing balance of their own masculine and feminine energies. When you **do not** see this growing balance **within the individuals and groups of individuals**, the original "ideals" invariably fall apart. **Domination and submission, overtly imposed or unconsciously agreed to,** take over the playing field, no matter how wonderful the ideals were to begin with.*

This seemed so true to me. Psychologically I have seen that what hurts people the most is to be overpowered by those they love and/or depend on, either by overt abuse or more pervasively by shame, judgment, intimidation, and abandonment. And of course I have seen it all over history, how a political, social or religious group, even when inspired by some ideal of common good– and certainly not all groups have originated from such inspiration– can so easily become an instrument of control, greed, suppression and extermination. And of course, I had seen it in myself more often than I could begin to recount. Whatever my stated philosophy of life might have been, I could not help but relate to myself *and others* as either one-up or one-down.

What was completely new to my understanding was that the **world theme** of Domination and Suppression originated from the Masculine/Feminine split and that healing for the human race is directly related to reuniting Masculine and Feminine energies in consciousness— starting with ourselves.

I was a long way from that healing. The Feminine in me had to come out from under lifetimes of destruction to come back into her own body, literally, in order to receive this great gift of the writing. The Masculine in me, which had finally asserted itself enough to get help, to get me out of a hurtful marriage, which kept speaking out with my daughter and as a therapist—that Masculine part of me had a lot more strength to gain if I was ever going to put out into the world the writing that the Feminine in me was receiving.

In my soul, I was in absolute awe of the magnitude of the understanding being conveyed. In my personality, I was just barely lifting myself out of the fire.

*We want to emphasize that the oppression of women and of feminine values, so widespread on earth today, is an issue **calling loudly to the potentially lethal outcome of this split if it goes on unchecked in the ego consciousness of the human race. What you want to understand, and this is why Mother Earth speaks to you so loudly, is that an assault on the Body of Woman and on the Feminine is an assault on the Body of Earth. Just as Woman is the carrier of life for ALL humans, male and female alike, Earth is the carrier of life for ALL OF YOU. Not only can you not Return without consciously embracing the re-union of Masculine and Feminine energies WITHIN YOURSELVES, you can no longer SURVIVE without embracing their re-union in action.***

*This was the challenge of the human race especially. Just as you personally might take on the challenge of being born into a life in which you must now speak your truth without fear and with your whole heart and soul, just so **the biggest challenge of the human race has been to be manifested in form as two different sexes and ultimately to consciously reunite the energies that have been divided**. The challenge is not to develop technology, it is not to tame Mother Nature, it is not to create wealth, and it is not to overcome mortality, though all these issues are certainly compelling AND related.*

*The main challenge, **which manifests in every issue the human race is dealing with, is to find a harmonious union of Assertion and Receptivity, Active Force and Generative Receiving.***

*This perfect balance is illustrated in the act of procreation and the generation of new life. The sperm penetrates the egg and the egg receives it. Together, **and only together**, they create new life. This is the principle of life for humans and for so many life forms on your planet. **CONSCIOUS PARTICIPATION IN THE RE-UNION OF MASCULINE AND FEMININE ENERGIES is the wisdom that is trying so hard to Push Through into awareness in the human race all over the world today,** no matter what the arena. You can see how much resistance there is to accepting this at the present time.*

*Your pattern of incarnations is not unlike that of many others. There is no particular distinction in it and that is not the purpose of bringing it into consciousness. **The true purpose of all past life work is to get a Reading on the World Theme that you, as one strand of creation, embody, and are working through to consciousness for the highest good of all.** There is no ego in this realm. It doesn't matter one iota if you were a king of Egypt or a slave in Mongolia. What matters is how close to Self you are able to stay and what learning for the rest of your fellow travellers you are able to contribute. The human race is a manifestation of a Divine Duality. Just as We told you about the Three in One—the Father, the Son, and the Holy Ghost– this issue of Masculine and Feminine (and all Duality) is the Two in the One. Masculine is essentially the force acting and Feminine is essentially the force (not entity) acted upon. Together they create new life— physically, psychologically, and spiritually. Together they have the power to manifest God on the earth plane over and over again.*

*God alone contains both the force acting and the force acted upon. In God, they are one. In mankind, they are two, two who must unite in order to replicate the divine act of creation. **You can see that the intense polarization between Masculine and Feminine results in greater and greater expressions of DESTRUCTION– NOT CREATION.** This can be seen in the production of weapons capable of mass extermination, the increasing attack, from a multitude of angles, on women's rights, gay rights, children's rights, animal rights, the rights of the poor, the rights of minorities, and in the destruction of the ecosystem.*

*When the Masculine/Feminine Duality is not understood and embraced consciously as **the challenge you humans came here to heal, to bring back to wholeness,** and especially now when the voice of the Feminine and the energy of Divine Receptivity is silenced by assault, degradation, and injustice **globally**, just as your personal voice and the voices of countless others have been silenced again and again, just as Mother Earth feels herself also being silenced– **then you have a greater and greater cry going out for Return—your personal cry, the cry of women and the oppressed everywhere, and the cry of Mother Earth.***

*It is in this vein that Mother earth speaks to you and to others. She is crying for the hurt being done to her body as you cry for the hurt done to yours. She is crying for the return of her brother and sister human beings to love **all** bodies—your bodies and her body for it is all one body. She is telling you to love your body as she loves hers. **Do you not see that this is the only way life on earth for you can continue?***

*Rape is lastingly devastating– for **both** the rapist and the one raped. Rape is the embodiment of an incredibly dense Horizontal Plane energy that has great power to keep that energy stuck on the Horizontal Plane. The effects on you, Phyllis, of the assault and powerlessness you experienced in childhood are what you are "Undoing" on your personal Road of Return. **On the Road of Return for all individuals and for the human race as a whole, the effects of one person or one group forcing their energy onto another person or group, or onto any other kingdom of creation, are exactly that which is CALLING OUT TO BE UNDONE.** THIS is the imbalance of Masculine and Feminine energies We are talking about.*

*Your particular path, like that of countless others, is to highlight and illuminate this truth. You have an interesting story on the personal level. But you see everyone does if they knew their story as you are coming to know yours. **Past life work that stops at the level of the personal interesting story has not done its full job, which is to illuminate the WORLD THEME FOR HUMANITY that you each*** *came here to Redeem for the Creator in such a way that the personal story is transcended or transformed for the rest of this particular round of time. We will say more about this later. For now, We will say that looking at the patterns and themes a person incarnates to experience and redeem through their many lives is a key to understanding what is needed in order to burn through Karma and become free of it. And in the biggest picture, it is a doorway to understanding one of the many themes the entire race is working through on the Road to Planetary Return—ALL OF WHICH can be accessed and furthered through the conscious work of balancing Masculine and Feminine energies within one's own being.*

All roads lead to this particular Rome for the human race. So you see, We are not talking just about men and women becoming aware of and manifesting an aspect of Divinity through their union, although that is certainly essential. We are talking about how a re-vision of the sacred re-union of Masculine/Feminine energies will impact not only the quality of human life but also the viability of the entire planet. No matter what Theme for the World a particular incarnated being is working on across the progression of lifetimes, they all culminate in the task of Union of the Two. They all culminate in union through equality, in union through the consent of equals. Divine Union cannot take place through unwanted penetration or possession of another's body, psyche, intellect, emotions, beliefs, abilities, home, or possessions. Therefore, all unwanted penetration of other, possession by force of other, is rape.

ALL oppressed people everywhere are the callers to this issue. The earth herself is a caller. Will you listen?

When one aspect of the Masculine/Feminine duality in a human being is injured, the other aspect cannot help but be out of balance in some way as well. As you work to energize the Feminine in you and the Mother from the Earth in you, the complementary Masculine is also awakened in you. For you right now this takes the form of a need to come out of hiding, the impulse to have a voice in the world. For each person, as soul awakens, the impulse to balance Masculine/Feminine energies within themselves will take its own personal form according to their soul path and pattern of energies.

*As We have said, if one aspect is not functioning properly or is injured, the other cannot function properly either. The other may be functioning forcefully but forcefully is not the same as properly. Properly means **in balance** with the other aspect. Therefore, regardless of whether a person inhabits a male or a female body, is heterosexual or gay, **this balance of masculine and feminine forces is the essence of the growth process.** We are not talking about appearances. We are not talking about anything external. We are talking about energizing and embodying a **balance** of Assertion and Receptivity within the psyche.*

*In your case, the history of your Soul's incarnations is filled with excessive force of the masculine used against the feminine, which **always takes the form of unwanted or unhealthy penetration on some level.** Physical rape is only one of thousands of forms that this unwanted or unhealthy penetration takes. The subliminal or overtly and deliberately distorted messages in the media would be an example of what We are talking about—deliberate lies used to manipulate and penetrate the psyches of listeners without true conscious consent. Governments and religious groups that rule by force, that impose their will through physical or economic or moral coercion— **no matter what principles or values they say they espouse**— if they rule by force they can only, in the end, contribute to the continued and intensified playing out of all the other dualities the human race struggles with— Good and Evil, Have and Have Not, Right and Wrong, Pleasure and Pain, Destruction and Creation, etc.– on the Horizontal Plane of existence. They can only contribute to the reinforcement of the Duality of Domination and Submission, the group in power always seeking to **impose its will** on another less powerful group and always seeking to strengthen the position that **keeps** them dominant.*

These themes are pervasive throughout human history. However, it is a mistake to blame this dynamic of the overuse of force on men. **We are not talking about blame here. We are shedding light on what has kept you as a race in the Karmic phase of your evolution. All that has played out through the Laws of Duality in human history is LAWFUL.** *The story of Adam and Eve is a symbolic representation of how the original SPLIT between Masculine and Feminine energies took hold in the human psyche. It is not a symbolic representation of original SIN. But that too is part of the Plan. We will say much more about this later.*

Your path exemplifies one particular aspect of this bigger struggle. **Each soul carries its own message in the form of one specific theme in the larger evolution of the Race of Man toward the reintegration or the re-union of these Two into One.** *In this evolutionary process, no personality is more important than any other. No soul is more important than any other. No message is more important than any other nor is it, in essence, any different from any other. When you look at Our Work from this perspective, you understand now why the Earth cries out in the way it does:* **That We all Return Together.**

Jesus embodied the perfect union of Masculine/Feminine energies. He was the **Receiver** *of Divine Love in his being and he was the* **Transmitter** *of that Divine Love to others on the Horizontal Plane. It is impossible for any truly evolved being to see the Feminine as inferior to the Masculine or to believe that the dynamic of domination and submission creates anything more than unending conflict– which lies at the heart of unparalleled global human suffering and the suffering of so many other living beings as well.*

The essence of the Path of the Earth is how Masculine and Feminine seek to reunite, and on that journey, the human race and all the individuals in it will be required to face and contend with all the beliefs they have taken on about themselves and "other" that keep them separate. *All life lessons and Paths are informed by this basic intent. The Shadow of the Holy Ghost is really the power* *inherent in ego consciousness to fuel the fire of Duality, to keep on creating "other," and thus fuel the fire of opposition in its many forms.*

This issue is not like a little stone in the road that you or anyone or the race of humans can somehow skip over. ***This is the road.***

*You see what is so sad about the state of the human race today is that the answer of what you are to do is right in front of you. What matters most for the human race, but which seems so difficult to grasp, is **the people themselves**, you and you and you—**ALL OF YOU**. **You** are the most important natural resource for yourselves, you are the most important friend for yourselves, you are the most important teacher for yourselves, **and your SURVIVAL is the most important reason to find this out now.***

Afterward

There is no good place to end this book. What is contained in these pages is just the very beginning of all They had to share with me. My journey continued to take me deeper into the past life that was opened up and into all the pain and darkness I still carried in my present life as well. In the process, so much more was revealed to me about our journey here on earth as soul in human form that there is no way to put it all into one book. This book really serves as an introduction.

I would like to give you an idea of what you will find in the books to come:

–More about the witch life

–More messages from the Earth

–Soul relationships and the Circles of Incarnation

– More about the Laws governing ego consciousness called the Laws of Gravity

–Supreme Surrender and The Breath of the Cross Meditation: the conversion of ego energy for use by Soul

–A new understanding of Adam and Eve

–The Astral Plane, Black and White Magic

–An outline of Soul's descent into human form and Light on the Road Home

–The Chakras and our Soul Path patterns understood through a configuration of Chakras called the Soul Triangle

–The Chakras of Humanity and the Chakras of the Earth planet

–The Rays of Creation and the Elements

–Christ Consciousness as the Soul of the Earth

–More about Jesus and what his appearance signified for Earth and for human evolution

–And all the while my personal journey taking me closer and closer to speaking all this out loud and the complications in my relationship with T that recapitulated my most difficult past life struggles

***

Thank you for taking this journey with me. I would like to end this first book with two of my favorite quotes from the writing:

Where is Judas now? Where are Pontius Pilate and his soldiers? Where is Salome? Think about this. Are they out there waiting for their final punishment, for the fire of Hell to descend on them in full view of the "faithful?" If so then the Church was right: there is a Hell and there is original sin. We think not. And you by now know that this is not where it all leads. You are all players in the same play and you are all going Home when that show is over, when God breathes the worlds back into himself. Whose role in the great unfolding of karma will you judge? Whose hand will you not take on the long road ahead? Whose baggage will you not help carry on the Road Home?

We all go Home together.

Contact The Author

Phyllis Leavitt can be contacted on her website at www.phyllisleavitt.com or by email at phyllisellenleavitt@ gmail.com.